D1614145

Living with fire

People, nature and history in Steels Creek

Christine Hansen & Tom Griffiths

CSIRO

PUBLISHING

National Library of Australia Cataloguing-in-Publication entry

Hansen, Christine.
Living with fire : people, nature and fire in Steels Creek
/ by Christine Hansen and Tom
Griffiths.

9780643104792 (hbk.)
9780643104808 (epdf)
9780643104815 (epub)

Includes index.

Black Saturday bushfires, 2009.
Wildfires – Social aspects – Victoria – Steels Creek.
Forest fires – Social aspects – Victoria – Steels Creek.
Steels Creek (Vic.) – Social life and customs.

Griffiths, Tom, 1957–

363.379099453

Published by
CSIRO PUBLISHING
150 Oxford Street (PO Box 1139)
Collingwood VIC 3066
Australia

Telephone: +61 3 9662 7666
Local call:1300 788 000 (Australia only)
Fax: +61 3 9662 7555
Email: publishing.sales@csiro.au
Web site: www.publish.csiro.au

Front cover: Looking into the Steels Creek valley from Yarra Ridge, May 2009
(photo by Christine Hansen)
Back cover: photo by Malcolm Calder
Inside front cover: The Millennium Quilt by the Steels Creek stitchers, launched March 2000
Inside back cover: The Phoenix Quilt by the Steels Creek stitchers, launched April 2012
Pages iii and iv: photos by Julia Fahey
Contemporary photographs are by the Steels Creek community and the authors unless otherwise indicated.

Royalties from the sale of this book go to the Steels Creek Community Centre Inc.

Set in Adobe Myriad Pro 10/16 and Minion Pro
Edited by Anne Findlay
Cover and text design by Andrew Weatherill
Typeset by Andrew Weatherill
Printed in China by 1010 Printing International Ltd

Original print edition:
The paper this book is printed on is in accordance with the rules of the Forest Stewardship Council®. The FSC® promotes environmentally responsible, socially beneficial and economically viable management of the world's forests.

MIX
Paper from
responsible sources
FSC
www.fsc.org   FSC® C016973

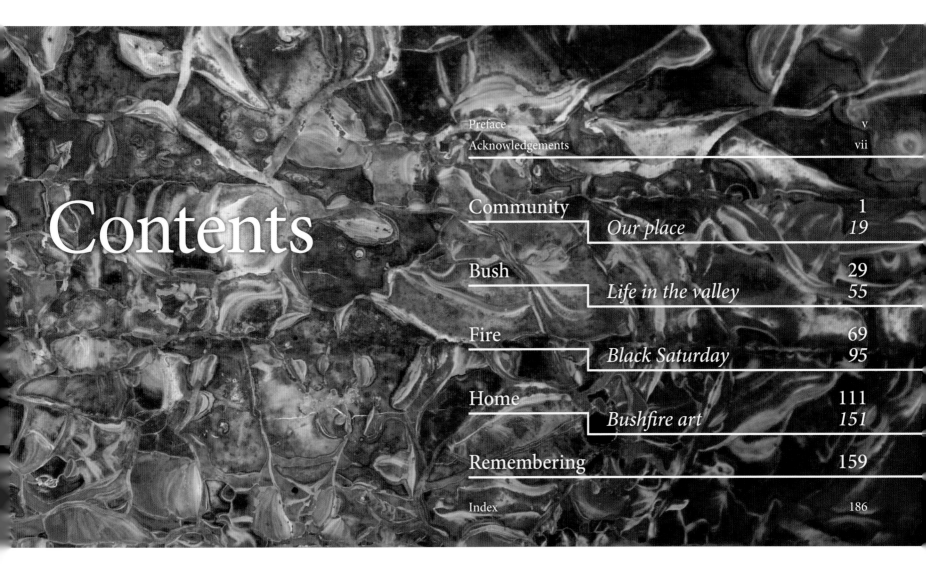

Contents

Preface

On 7 February 2009, Steels Creek – a small community in the Yarra Valley of Victoria – lost 10 lives and two-thirds of its homes in the Black Saturday firestorm. This book is first and foremost for the people of Steels Creek. We hope it will contribute to your understanding of the history of your valley and help to make sense of what happened on Black Saturday. The book is also for other Australian communities that live with fire. Here are stories of how the people of one valley are coming to terms with the greatest elemental force shaping Australian settlement.

Living with Fire is written by two historians with the collaboration, help and guidance of Steels Creek residents. Both historians have a strong association with the Yarra Ranges through growing up in Melbourne's eastern suburbs with the blue hills on the horizon and making weekend trips to the green river flats and tall trees. Christine lived for a time in Kinglake West in Coombs Road (where the Black Saturday fire was so deadly) and spent many long Saturdays at the St Andrews market and the Kinglake pub. Tom wrote a history of the region called *Forests of Ash* and often visited Steels Creek friends, Malcolm and Jane Calder, after they came to live in the valley in the late 1980s. Tom's children, Kate and Billy, quietly picked and ate most of the cherry tomatoes in Malcolm and Jane's garden at Blackwood Hill during one especially rewarding visit in the early 1990s.

After Black Saturday Malcolm wrote to Tom about *how we might work to achieve a really worthwhile community benefit from the apparent disaster. We have lost friends, friends have lost homes and the community is still in shock. There needs to be a project to understand the community experience, the community response and the way forward to the future.* The people of the small, dispersed settlement of Steels Creek have never had much public infrastructure and so their communal needs following the fire were primarily social and intellectual. They wanted answers to the following questions: What *exactly* happened on the day? How did people die and how did they survive? What does 'community' mean in such a crisis and how does it work – or not? What is the emotional aftermath of the event and how are survivors reinventing their lives and their places? What does it mean to rebuild, knowing that your house may be vaporised at some time in the next generation? What kind of society evolves in conditions where investment in material culture is so insecure? Perhaps it is a society that invests instead in social capital and historical consciousness, in the sinews and fabric of community, in the capacity to put life ahead of property.

This book is one product of a three-year research project with Steels Creek people that has explored those questions. As well as *Living with Fire,* our project has also germinated Peter Stanley's *Black Saturday at Steels Creek: Fire and an Australian Community* (2013) and Moira Fahy's documentary film that follows the experience of three families since the fire. Whereas the focus of Peter's book is Black Saturday itself and Moira's film its emotional aftermath, *Living with Fire* aims to place the experience of Black Saturday in the context of the long environmental and social history of the valley, and it thus considers the challenge of cultural adaptation. We hope the book will find its way onto every kitchen table in the valley and into the homes of other Australians living in or near the bush. We hope also that it might encourage fire scholars and managers to work closely with fire-prone communities and to think about bushfire in ways that are more local, ecological and historical.

Christine Hansen
Tom Griffiths

Acknowledgements

We thank the people of Steels Creek for sharing their stories with us. It has been a great privilege to work with them on the history of their valley.

Malcolm and Jane Calder have generously given us guidance, wisdom, hospitality and friendship throughout this entire project. Helen Mann of the Yarra Glen & District Historical Society assisted our research with her deep knowledge of local history. Christine Mullen and Chris Grikscheit helped us to find, and work with, many of the artists in the valley. Malcolm, Jane, Helen, Christine and Chris made it possible for us to hold several community workshops that generated ideas, images, stories and art that appear in the interludes or visual essays of this book.

Moira Fahy, Peter Stanley, Emily O'Gorman, Cameron Muir, Rob Buckell and Ingereth Macfarlane shared the research and fieldwork with us. We are very grateful for the stimulus of their conversations and the insights of their research.

So many residents of the valley, past and present, have contributed to this book that it is impossible to name them all. But we would like to acknowledge especially the support and encouragement of Hannah Sky, who has done so much to capture local stories, and Barbara Hunt Harris and Meryl Collinson who generously shared their family histories and community memories. Others who have generously supported this project, provided us with stories and photos and welcomed us in their homes include: David and Robyn Allan;

Rudi and Shirley Anders; Dorothy Barber; Nicole, Samantha and Ellie Beecroft; Frances and Gordon Brown; James and Morgan Calder; Andrew Chapman; Margaret Crozier; Ray and Bronwyn Dahlstrom; Sandra de Pury and Gilbert de Pury of Yeringberg, Coldstream; Rob and Julie Fallon; Sally Ferres and Dave Gormly; Margaret and John Houston; Angie and Graham Lloyd; Mary Mann; Craig and Eva Matthews; Margaret and Richard McLoughlin; Keith and Lindy Montell; Erin-Marie O'Neill and John Brand (and Henry); Frank Orenshaw; Max Scott; Barry Sheffield; Barry Smith; John Sutton; Dave Twentyman; Pam Verhoeven; John Walker; Mike Watkins; and Edd and Amanda Williams.

When we began this project, we were given access to a box of documents, photos, clippings, notes and interview transcripts that were gathered by members of the Steels Creek community in the decade before the fire with the aim of writing their local history. We pay tribute to the late Eric Tetlow who was the prime mover behind this initiative to research a history of Steels Creek. That archive of documents, supplemented by the products of our own research, now forms the Steels Creek Community Archive held by the Yarra Glen & District Historical Society.

James Calder and ACME Et Al Photographics have supported this book with superb reproduction of historical photos and contemporary artwork. James Calder's own fine photography is represented throughout. Unless otherwise indicated, contemporary photographs are by the Steels Creek community and the authors. Julia Fahey kindly made her photos available for this book. We also thank the local artists whose work is included in this volume: Nicole,

Samantha and Ellie Beecroft, Margaret Brewster, Jane Calder, Malcolm Calder, Michael Dahlstrom, Ray Dahlstrom, Deva Daricha, Ivan Filsell, Chris Grikscheit, Robyn Henchel, Margaret Houston, Margaret McLoughlin, Richard McLoughlin, Christine Mullen and Noel Nicolson.

Our sincere thanks go to those who read drafts of part or all of the manuscript: Jane Calder, Malcolm Calder, Meryl Collinson, Moira Fahy, Malcolm Gill, Billy Griffiths, Barbara Hunt Harris, Grace Karskens, Ingereth Macfarlane, Helen Mann, Cameron Muir, Libby Robin, Hannah Sky, Peter Stanley, and Kevin Tolhurst.

We are grateful to the following institutions for their permission to reproduce photographs or documents: the Yarra Glen and District Historical Society, the Healesville Library, the Forests Commission Retired Personnel Association (especially Rod Incoll), the State Library of Victoria and the National Library of Australia. We also thank the Yarra Ranges Shire Council and the Yarra Glen Grand Hotel for their assistance. Crucial support for the project has been provided by the School of History and the Centre for Environmental History at the Australian National University, the Centre for Historical Research at the National Museum of Australia, and the Cultural Heritage Initiative of Gothenburg University, Sweden.

Financial support for the Steels Creek project (including the film) was generously provided by the Thomas Foundation, the Sidney Myer Fund, the Vice-Chancellor of the Australian National University, the Office of Emergency Services Commissioner, Victoria; the Fire Services Commissioner, Victoria;

the Department of Sustainability and Environment, Victoria; the Country Fire Authority of Victoria, the Victorian Bushfire Reconstruction and Recovery Authority, the Bushfire Cooperative Research Centre, the Victorian Premier's Alfred Deakin Prize, and the artist Mandy Martin. We gratefully acknowledge the support and encouragement of Bruce Esplin, Craig Lapsley, Euan Ferguson and Ewan Waller.

We feel very fortunate indeed to have been able to work with the gifted and devoted team at CSIRO Publishing led by John Manger. John believed in this book from its inception and we thank him for his vision and encouragement. Pilar Aguilera, Tracey Millen, Melinda Chandler, Anne Findlay and designer Andrew Weatherill have all enhanced the book. They share our belief that this is both a regional history and a parable for all communities that live with fire.

Christine Hansen & Tom Griffiths

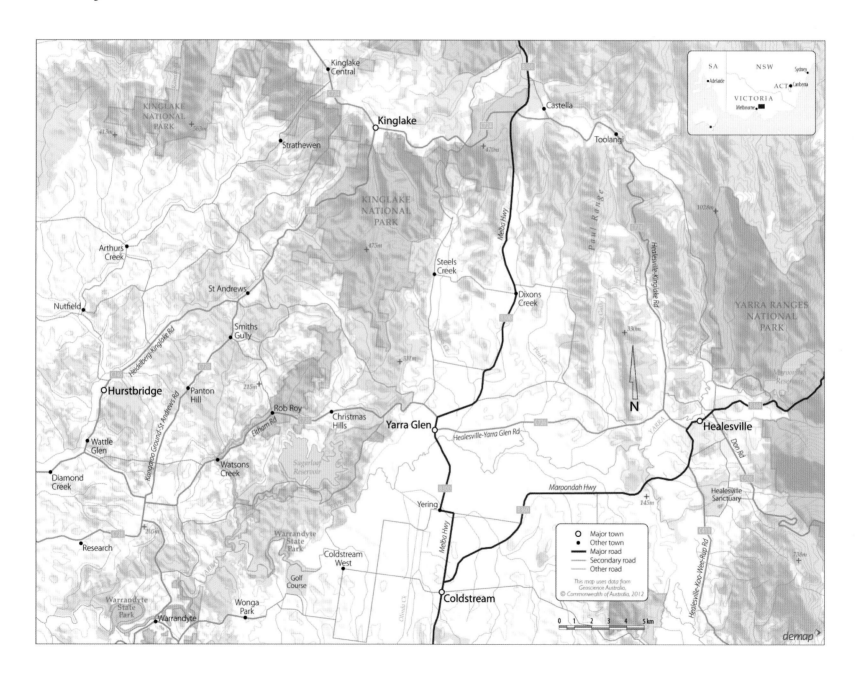

Community

Christine Hansen

Ivan Filsell, 'Three generations at work', 2011.

The first Saturday following the devastating fires of February 2009 was an assigned market day. The valley was holding its breath after the firestorm that had exploded out of the surrounding bushland just seven days before. Smoke was still hanging in a hazy layer on the horizon and rumours of destruction swirled in eddies, mixing with the charred remains. Who had succumbed? Who had survived? What had been lost? What had been saved? Miraculously (with some help from the team of Ivan Filsell, his son and grandson), the wooden Community Centre was still standing when every tree and blade of grass surrounding it was gone. Discussions about whether to hold the market or not brought focus to the confusion of that first week, as people struggled without access to basic amenities such as clean water, phones and power,

or to find clothing and accommodation for those who had lost everything. Would it be insensitive to carry on as usual? Organisers decided to go ahead with their plans. The community, they reasoned, needed a place to gather together: to meet neighbours and friends, hear news of who had perished, who had lost their house, their livelihood, their pets, their gardens; to share the first exhalation of breath as the chaos and terror of the firestorm began a slow and painful retreat into the past.

As market day dawned, people still black with ash, many struggling to find enough clothes to make a public appearance, began arriving at the Community Centre. Car after car lined up for a space on the grassy verge. Still in shock, the valley residents emerged into the charred landscape to present themselves to each other, living evidence of their survival. People dug deep to find an object to exchange at the 'market'; a bunch of charred flowers here and a few blackened potates there, all a determined reminder of life.

Regular market days usually attracted between 30 and 40 people; it's more about swapping news than buying the jars of homemade jams and pickles for sale. The Saturday after the fires, however, the crowd swelled to almost 200 at its peak, a record in the 20-year history of the market.[1] Much-needed information circulated; some brought reports of missing neighbours who had fled before the storm and were staying with relatives; some knew of others seeking treatment in the city; some had hair-raising tales of a close escape; some had lost their home; some had returned to put down animals too badly injured to survive; some were still too dazed to speak but needed the balm of company. Most shocking of all was news of those who had perished, the worst in the long list of losses. Over the following days and weeks, as the smoke lifted and the clearing of debris began, the terrible picture of what had occurred came into sharper focus: 10 people died; 67 houses burnt to the ground leaving more than 250 people homeless;[2] an untallied number of pets and farm animals perished and an unimaginable number of native birds and animals – many of them much-loved wild friends of the valley community – were killed.

On this first Saturday, as the crowd of neighbours and friends milled in and around the little schoolhouse, they shared their shock, grief and relief in equal measure, drawing together in a spontaneous gesture of community: the people of Steels Creek.

* * *

Steels Creek is not so much a place as an attitude. At least that's the description offered by president of the Steels Creek Community Centre at the time of the fires, Keith Montell. 'The relationship between infrastructure and community, between material things and people, is different here … A lot of people have asked since the fire: "How do you define Steels Creek?" I say: "It's a state of mind. If you want to be here, you're welcome."' Driving the length of Steels Creek Road as it travels along the valley floor, you get a sense of what he means. Just 10 km from end to end, this picturesque country avenue follows the north–south line of the creek from its plunge off the escarpment of the Great Dividing Range in the north to its convergence with the Yarra River in the south. Although clearly marked on the map as a locality, there is no marker to tell the passing tourist they have arrived, save the 'Welcome to Steels Creek' sign that straddles a roadside culvert at a seemingly random location.

Despite the lack of material definition, the people of Steels Creek determinedly pursue their idea of community. It is shared interests and group activities that bring them together and the old schoolhouse is the hub around which the goings-on revolve. When the school closed in 1992, locals mounted a fierce campaign to wrest control of the building from the state government. Twenty years on the appreciation of that struggle has not diminished. Serving as a meeting room, talks hall, picture theatre, gallery, plant propagation area,

1   Steels Creek Community Notes in *The Jolly Thing*, No. 86 (August–September 2010).
2   These figures are compiled from local records with the assistance of Linda Leckie, Building Services, Yarra Ranges Shire Council.

marketplace, art studio, sewing room, picnic area and even on occasion as a field laboratory, the little weatherboard and corrugated iron building holds the vision of community in place. In April 2012 a new extension to the Community Centre was opened.

Not everyone in Steels Creek participates in the idea of valley life that flows through the Community Centre, however, and people often express delicate feelings about inclusion and exclusion. Not surprisingly. There is a distinct demographic flavour to the group who keep the activities alive, although they more than any are aware of the 'insider' and 'outsider' sensitivities and are at pains to insist that they don't define the community. Most have arrived from the suburbs of Melbourne, bringing with them self-funded retirement income, capital from real estate divestment or resources to start up niche businesses. With a metropolitan railway line just 20 km away and a six-lane freeway leading to the heart of Melbourne starting not far beyond, some still commute to the city for work. A new generation work at home using technology to 'telecommute'. Others spend weekdays in a *pied-à-terre* in town, returning to the valley for weekends, although they nominate Steels Creek as their primary home. Still others enjoy their 'weekender' when time permits, and have done so for more than two decades. Whatever their circumstances, the idea of 'belonging' is important to this group and the way in which they make an effort to belong adds complexity and often expertise to the local mix.

Steels Creek has lent itself to this type of demographic expansion over the last three or four decades for a number of reasons: its location in relation to the city,

its setting along the border of Kinglake National Park, an area of great natural beauty, and its proximity to two large universities at the north-eastern and north-western edges of outer Melbourne play significant roles. Many in the first wave of 'tree-changers' to the valley in the 1980s were academics and many of those specialised in natural sciences. To the extent that they were educated and, by local standards at least, well heeled, these new arrivals reflected the interests of people in peri-urban areas around the developed world. The 1980s was a time of social reorientation when many disillusioned city dwellers looked for alternatives to the fast-paced, high-consumption lifestyle on offer. Australians were no exception. An existing love of the outdoors and a proud do-it-yourself culture helped the social revolution of the previous decades find form in a momentum towards country living. City dwellers searched for locations where they might make their dream of a 'return to the land' and an increased self-sufficiency became a reality. A coincidence in global trade circumstances helped them along. When Australian dairy exports to the United Kingdom ceased almost overnight in the mid-1970s many small farms failed, leaving large tracts of farmland close to the city vacant. A generation ready to adopt an alternative lifestyle took advantage of the opportunity. Everywhere along the populated coastal fringes of Australia large acreage farms were divided into smaller lots or bought for multiple occupancy developments. The areas surrounding Steels Creek in the upper Yarra Valley and nearby districts were some of the first to transform. Christmas Hills, Panton Hills, Kangaroo Ground, Arthurs Creek, Hurstbridge and St Andrews became centres where alternative communities flourished, renowned for their adaptive mud brick architecture as much as for their self-sufficiency ambitions and desire for community.

Although on the edge of the main 'mud brick belt', the valley of Steels Creek attracted its share of urban refugees. The gentle vistas to the east, the dramatic escarpment to the west and north, the protected bushland of the adjacent national park and the opportunity to own 'some space' made the valley an attractive destination. In return, the new arrivals brought a welcome wave of energy into a flagging economy. Unlike other areas of the Yarra Valley, Steels Creek had never been a site of flourishing primary production, despite its appearance of abundance. Some of the soils provide good drainage, but are too deficient in nutrients to support much pasture and the few farms that did exist were mainly fruit orchards growing crops that enjoyed poorer conditions. Financially independent of the local economy, the new arrivals were free to choose land for reasons other than its production potential: outlooks to the surrounding countryside, extant native bush, the gurgling creek, proximity to the national park and so on. Blocks of land on the ridges and escarpment that were worthless as farms suddenly became ideal 'lifestyle' properties, many of them with panoramic views across the Great Dividing Range. Where not long before 100 acres was barely enough, suddenly 20-acre blocks were becoming the norm.

As the idea of the rural retreat settled into the aspirations of mainstream Australia during the decades following the 1980s, those who had already made the transition sought to connect with the places and people that now surrounded them. Locals produced newspapers and newsletters (including Steels Creek's *The Jolly Thing*, the now online community information sheet whose title came from an editor's worries about how to get people 'to read the jolly thing'); set up farmers' markets and food cooperatives; founded artists' studios; and craft groups, skills workshops, reading groups, film clubs and information sessions all became regular fixtures on local calendars in small town Australia. Steels Creek, with its ready-made meeting space and its educated population, was ripe for such a flourishing and a lively local culture took root. Over the years the pulse of community in the valley settled into a seasonal rhythm; the time for planting, the time for pruning; the time for planning, the time for doing. The gentle pace of valley life ebbed and flowed, with activities following the course of the year: walking groups in the cooler months, an art show in the autumn, barbeques in the summer evenings, open gardens in the spring.

But the wave of urban migrants that arrived in the valley did not arrive into an empty landscape. A local community with long traditions was already in place. Some valley dwellers were descendants of settler families that had made their mark on the landscape over a century before. Some were tradespeople, service industry staff, council workers and farmhands, attracted to the area for family or economic reasons. Some had small businesses that depended on the local economy for survival. And not everyone was happy with the new arrivals. As the tide of people moving from the city reached the valley, cultural and political diversity followed. Inevitably occasional tensions flared as ideas, tastes and values came into conflict. Today Steels Creek is anything but monocultural, yet even if the occasional class or culture clash erupts, variety among the valley dwellers is usually easily accommodated. It is part of the charm of the place and one of the reasons it inspires such loyalty.

Local knowledge and a sense of shared experience are other factors that bring people together. The tracks and trails along which people live their lives are carved not just into the landscape but into personal histories. Local knowledge is won from experience and observation. It is inherited from families, passed on through neighbours, dug for in archives. It is exchanged in the carpark of the supermarket, at the bar of the pub, at the bowser of the petrol station, at the drop-off line of the school. The witnessing of time, the investment of self and the relationships within the community are the strands that bind people to the landscape and it is within this weave that a sense of place is formed. Perhaps that is why the fires of Black Saturday were felt as a betrayal by so many. For people who had invested so deeply in this place, the violent rending of this intimate social fabric was personal and challenged their confidence that they knew and understood their habitat. The deep grooves along which people travel – to work, to the city, to school, to social and sporting events, to visit friends and neighbours – and the experience and memories that are located within those pathways, conspire to give an impression of inevitability to this place. It feels real, fully formed, more than just a social construction or the accumulation of ideas and histories. But there is nothing inevitable about these layers of history. Each is the result of a moment, an era, an action that has left its particular and unique trace.

* * *

Hoogies Hardware in Yarra Glen, at the mouth of the Steels Creek valley, is a one-stop-shop for all your rural needs. Its unmissable roadside sign declaring 'Hoogies – No Worries' on the edge of town clears up any queries you might

have had about the contemporary local economy, with their purple and green logo depicting a hammer, some planks of milled timber and a bunch of grapes. This is wine country, no doubt about it. Further down the road, the Steels Creek turn-off is littered with signs for B&Bs and cellar door sales. A drive along the road takes you into the patchwork of vineyards that decorate the slopes rising from the valley as the view opens to a postcard-perfect vista of vines stretching in grids towards the horizon in the east. Some of the vineyards are owned by large corporate wine producers, some are just a few acres tended by families for their own use or for sale to local vignerons to crush for boutique vintages. Of course, where there is good wine, good food tends to follow and the upper Yarra Valley is happy to provide. Breads, pastries, cheeses, cured meats, preserves, condiments, confectionary, ice cream, roasted coffee and specialty teas are all produced locally, aimed at the increasingly sophisticated tastes of visitors from Melbourne and beyond.

These days the upper Yarra Valley 'foodie' tourist trail leads weekend gourmands along Steels Creek Road in increasing numbers. With so few reminders of the past still visible in the landscape, however, visitors may not realise they are following well-worn tracks. They might be surprised to learn for instance that their *bon vivant* forebears were quaffing the local produce as early as 1845, when grapes from vines planted seven years before at Yering by the adventuring Ryrie brothers were crushed for the first local vintage. Why the Scottish lads thought it a good idea to pack vine cuttings in their saddlebags at the start of their many-month trek southwards across the Snowy Mountains to the Yarra Valley is anyone's guess. Even more curious is how they managed to keep the tender young plants alive, when their first priority must surely have been to the 250 head of cattle they were droving across the highest mountain range in Australia.[3] No doubt they gave the job of nurseryman to one of the four convict stockmen they brought with them. The brothers had carefully selected two grape varieties to carry, the Black Cluster of Hamburg and a white grape called Sweetwater, although there had been plenty to choose from. By the time the Ryries were packing their bags, the canny entrepreneurs John and Elizabeth Macarthur were offering 33 different seedling varieties for sale from their Camden Park Estate Nursery, 70 km south-west of Sydney. For those who could afford it, wine was the drink of the day in the mid-19th century and there was a growing market for local product that could sidestep the high costs of importation. William, Donald and James Ryrie clearly gained inspiration from the experiments that had been carried out in the Sydney basin. The 1800 litres of wine Gregory Blaxland had shipped to London, for example, had won the coveted Gold Ceres Medal at the Royal Society of Arts.[4] If the venture went well, there was money to be made. Sadly, it was not an entirely successful experiment. Although they stumbled into a perfect environment for growing grapes, their flourishing vines did not lead to anything drinkable and opinion about their winemaking skills was not complimentary, despite the intervention of expert vigneron James Dardel. As wine producers, the brothers made great cattle farmers.

Scene at Yering – gathering grapes *H.L. van den Houten 1875. An early depiction of the Ryrie property on the Upper Yarra River, not far from the Steels Creek confluence. The vineyards are in the foreground, behind the building.[5]*

Today the Ryries are celebrated locally not as pioneers of the wine industry but as the first white men to set up camp in the area. This is the layer of history where the story most often begins; the time 'before the Ryries' is considered prehistory – the domain of archaeology or even early anthropology. This moment of beginning, however, belongs exclusively to the immigrants for whom it was a moment of arrival; for the Indigenous people already living in the valley and surrounding areas it was a moment of interruption. Whatever

3   Andrews AEJ (1998). Earliest Monaro and Burragorang, 1790 to 1840: with Wilson, Bass, Barrallier, Caley, Lhotsky, Jauncey, Lambie, Ryrie. Palmerston, Tabletop Press, ACT.

4   Norrie P (1990) *Vineyards of Sydney – Cradle of the Australian Wine Industry from First Settlement to Today.* Horwitz Grahame Pty Ltd, Sydney.

5   State Library of Victoria Accession No: H29754 Image No: b28605.

direction they were travelling from, however, the two tribes – the immigrants and the locals – met and engaged, and that moment has left deep traces. The refined cattlemen instincts of the Ryrie brothers led them to a house site a mile or two from the entrance to the Steels Creek valley in 1838 and before long they had taken up a grazing licence on a huge 43 000 acre run. The name they chose for their property 'Yering', means 'scrubby bush' in the local Woiwurrung language. *Yering* is no random selection but a word that accurately describes the type of marshland they nominated for their house site.[6] There must have been a conversation of sorts with the local people, maybe even a sustained friendship, for this word to have crossed the border into the immigrant world. Perhaps a few supplies were shared, a trade of tools or even chitchat about the weather: if there is any topic that can bridge the gap between farmers of different backgrounds, it's the weather. But it was hard for the newcomers to hear the cadences and rhythms of the old language with any real understanding. Although the Ryries took on the word *yering* as the name of their property, other clues were missed and the opportunity to base their new lives on millennia of Wurundjeri local knowledge was lost.

If the Ryries' linguistic curiosity laid down the first layer of immigrant history, the next was marked on maps and pegged on the ground by the first title holders of the Steels Creek valley – Mr John Dickson (for whom the next-door valley of Dixons Creek is named) who soon after sold it to Mr William Bell and his brother-in-law and business partner Mr Thomas Armstrong.[7] There would be no experiments with grapes for these gents. They were happy to leave the experiments in wine growing to the minor Swiss aristocrats who had taken over the vineyards at Yering from the Ryrie Brothers (and who subsequently met with huge success).[8] The Steels Creek valley, however, would have made a perfect free-range cattle pen and the rumour persists that the first generation of squatters made use of it. Not more than a half day's ride from end to end, with an escarpment on two sides, clean water in the creek and native grasses on the flatlands, the valley needed only a rudimentary fence across the southern end to secure the stock in a perfectly appointed 'paddock'. Strictly sheep and cattle men, Bell and Armstrong set about stocking their property with herds of valuable European breeds, as well as their much-loved Clydesdale horses. The animals were both ties to their homelands, the core of the farming practices they knew so well, and the foundations from which to grow the fortunes they hoped for in the new land.

The marshy Wurundjeri country these early immigrants found themselves in was no doubt strange in many ways, but the farming of sheep and cattle was a cultural and economic touchstone that anchored them from the start. Focused by concern for their animals, the strangeness of the environment would have quickly reduced to matters of grazing potential, water location and other much chewed-over farming lore. It was the animals themselves that straddled the real border between the known and unknown. As they took their first steps along the valley floor, the hard hooves of the cattle would have bitten into the silty soil, so different from the soft pads of the marsupials whose tracks threaded through the bush. As the sheep snuffled and nibbled at the grasses and seeds, they would have trampled the tubers of the *Microseris lanceolata*, the nutritious yam

---

6   Woiwood M (2010) *The Christmas Hills Story: Once Around the Sugarloaf II*. Andrew Ross Museum, Kangaroo Ground, Victoria.

7   Williams A (1996) *Steels Creek: Vineyards, Landscape and Development*. University of Melbourne, Melbourne, p. 26.

8   The descendants of these Swiss immigrants, the de Pury family, still own one of the original vineyards and are still making award-winning wine in the valley today.

daisy that grows along the creek banks, known by the Woiwurrung as *murnong*, a vital element of the local diet. They would have pulled at the clusters of *Poa labillardieri*, the tussock grass known as *bowat*, an important resource for making string used for weaving nets, bags, baskets and mats. They would have knocked against the giant *Dicksonia antarctica*, the old soft tree ferns growing at the end of the valley, known as *kombadik* with their delicious soft, starchy middle that could be scooped out from the top of the stem for eating cooked or raw.[9]

The Wurundjeri must have watched in disbelief as these lumbering monsters trampled their gardens and ruined their water sources. And we can be certain they were watching. If there was one thing the Woiwurrung knew, it was what was happening on their country. The first of the Ryries' cattle might have wandered into the valley during the cool rainy days of *waring*, or wombat season, of 1838, just the right time of year for them to adjust to their new surroundings.[10] Perhaps the families who enjoyed custodian rights to this country were away from the valley at the time, camping in a more open area on the Yarra River floodplains. As the contemporary community knows too well, *waring* can be hard some years, with the bone-chilling mist clinging to the creek long after sunrise. Perhaps the families returned when the weather had warmed up around *buath gurru* or grass flowering season, when the new growth attracted game. What must they have made of the trampled yam beds and chewed grasses they would have found on their return? Of the cow dung fouling the water? Of the strange lowing and lumbering beasts that now ruled the valley?[11]

* * *

The layers of history that have come and gone in Steels Creek are not easy to see. In this fire-adapted country it is the absences that create the layers as much as what remains. Here local knowledge holds the past in place: memories of where the family homes stood, the old shop, the farm sheds and barns, all long gone. The Black Saturday fires have added another ghosted layer to this absent past. Within weeks of the 2009 fires, Steels Creek Road hummed with the drone of heavy equipment. Front-end loaders and cranes, chainsaws and mulchers clanged and buzzed as burnt debris was mounded into heaps and carted off to the tip in semi-trailers. Residents who had lost so much were distraught to see the melted and charred remains of their homes so quickly displaced. Most had no opportunity to sift the wreckage for mementoes or scavenge for materials that could be incorporated into their new houses before the sites had been scraped clean ready to begin anew. Suddenly, still raw from the trauma of their loss, people were thrust into a new building project with little preparation. Now they were being asked to make decisions about windows and carpets and bathroom tiles, or worse, struggle with council approvals and tradespeople and rain as the building of new dwellings began. Many reported that they were overwhelmed by the process.

9   De Angelis D (2005) *Aboriginal Use Plants of the Greater Melbourne Area*. La Trobe University Environment Collective. See also: Gott B and Zola N (1992) *Koorie Plants, Koorie People: Traditional Aboriginal Food, Fibre and Healing Plants of Victoria*. Koorie Heritage Trust, Melbourne; Museum Victoria (2001) *Aboriginal Plant Use*. Information Sheet No. 10319; Kuranga Native Nursery *Bush Foods: Edible Plants from the Greater Melbourne Area*.

10 All information on the Kulin Calendar comes from Museum Victoria 'Tall Forests' exhibition. Also see Allen L 'Coranderrk Calendar' (2001). In *Forests of Ash: An Environmental History*. (Ed. T Griffiths) , Cambridge University Press, Melbourne, pp. 58–59.

11 Blackburn L (1996) *Yarra Valley Aborigines*. Local History Series. Lilydale & District Historical Society; Brough Smyth R (1878) *The Aborigines of Victoria*. Vol. 1. J. Ferres, Government Printer, Melbourne.

Building a house might have been an unwanted experience for many Steels Creek residents, but in beginning anew they were participating in an age-old tradition, what had once been a regular job for the Wurundjeri. The Aboriginal families who occupied the Yarra Ranges country at various times of the year lived in huts made from local timbers and bark. Constructed in the shape of a tent or erected as a lean-to, depending on the season, they made use of the excellent resources immediately to hand. To European eyes the Aboriginal camps looked primitive and randomly assembled. In reality they were sophisticated shelters that caught or deflected prevailing winds, protected from rain and captured warmth from evening fires at the same time as repelling smoke. Both the substantial crossbeam and the thick sheets of bark that provided the skin of the building often survived for many years, but in seasons of big water and big fire nobody worried about saving them: they could be made again quickly and easily when the families returned later in the year – to raise an entire complex of buildings and shelters took just an hour or so. This was architecture perfectly adapted to the environment. Intentionally ephemeral, the buildings offered seasonally adapted protection while making no demands to be defended against the great tides of fire and water that overtook the ridges and valleys in certain seasons.[12]

F. Kruger. Mid or late 1880s. Aboriginal family outside 'Mia Mia' – Coranderrk, Victoria.[13]

Bush Hut, Gippsland *postcard circa 1904.*[14]

12   Memmot P (2007) *Gunyah Goondie + Wurley: The Aboriginal Architecture of Australia.* University of Queensland Press, St Lucia, Qld.

13   State Library of NSW Call Number: At Work and Play – 05976.

14   State Library of Victoria Accession No: H90.25/141 Image No: a05205.

The early settlers would not have conceived of their buildings as ephemeral in quite the same way, yet their camps looked remarkably similar to those of the Wurundjeri. The Ryries' first dwelling was probably made of unstripped timber uprights with stringybark for walls, perhaps supplemented with a scrap or two of canvas. Luckily the sheets of local stringybark lasted well and clearly they made a good job of building their 'temporary' digs. Nineteen months after their arrival in the valley, Governor La Trobe visited the Ryries and reported that big brother William was still 'living in his old hut at the time'.[15] Their neighbour, Mr Bell, also made use of what was to hand. He built an entire farm complex of more than 10 buildings using timber cleared from his land as he wrestled the valley floor into open pasture during the 1850s. The slab constructions, with peeled logs used as structural members and roofs of split shingles, were anything but ephemeral. Remarkably, some of the original timber farm buildings are still standing today, having dodged countless bushfires in the past 170 years through a combination of good luck and great care. These marvellous old structures are now considered important cultural heritage and Gulf Station is part of the National Trust estate. The complex was valiantly defended by local firefighters in 2009.

What the Ryries, the Bells, the Armstrongs, the Wurundjeri and all the other locals either already knew or quickly discovered was that the forests of Steels Creek, and of the Yarra Valley and Great Dividing Range more widely, were a fantastic resource. The grand old stands of messmate or *Eucalyptus obliqua*, known in Woiwurrung language as *wangnarra*, had not just provided timber for housing but tinder for fire making and fibre for string bags and fishing nets for at least 2000 generations. The white skinned manna gums (*Eucalyptus viminalis* or *binnap* in Woiwurrung) that followed the line of the creek had likewise fed, housed and healed their custodians for millennia with smoke from the leaves used to reduce fever and the sugary white extrusions used as a delicious sweet treat.[16] The newcomers to the valley soon followed the example of the Wurundjeri, finding that the great sheets of stiff fibrous bark that could be prised off the messmate made a wonderful roofing material, lasting upwards of 30 years if well maintained. The tall timber, sometimes reaching over 80 metres in height, with its straight grain and attractive colour was similarly perfect for use in construction. With a burgeoning city just down the river, such riches were not going to stay secret for long. By the time the professional timber-getters' sights settled on the Steels Creek valley, Melbourne was desperate for building materials, and for a reason no-one saw coming.

On 1 July 1851, Melbourne's residents celebrated their separation from New South Wales with a series of parties, balls and official receptions. As they donned their best clothes and opened their finest wine (including, no doubt, a drop of the vastly improved Yering vintage) to toast the birth of the Colony of Victoria, the 29 000 citizens of this bustling southern port had no idea of what was about to hit them: just days later gold was found. At first it was an exciting but modest find of alluvial gold at Clunes, followed by a fairly substantial find at Warrandyte. By the time the third find was made at Ballarat, all within just one month, rumours and tall tales were flying fast and furious: stories of nuggets lying on the ground, of creeks and rivers sparkling with gold dust, of vast veins as thick as a man's arm just waiting to be mined circulated

15   Woiwood M (2010) *The Christmas Hills Story: Once Around the Sugarloaf II*, p. 8.

16   Zola N, Gott B and Koorie Heritage Trust (1992) *Koorie Plants, Koorie People: Traditional Aboriginal Food, Fibre and Healing Plants of Victoria*. Koorie Heritage Trust, Melbourne.

around the colonies. When a report about the finds was published in the *Argus* on 8 September 1851, a massive rush to pocket a share of the world's newest and richest goldfield began. Within a year 75 000 people had arrived to seek their fortune. So sudden was the tide of immigrants and so critical was the shortage of accommodation that a tent city, known as 'Canvas Town' was established at South Melbourne to house more than 10 000 new arrivals. It soon became a massive slum. By 1890 the population of Melbourne had swollen to a colossal half a million making it, at least for a time, the largest city in the British Empire after London. The population explosion and the enormous wealth being extracted from the goldfields fuelled a boom that lasted for 40 years.[17]

To house its new citizens, rather than building high-density apartment blocks like European cities, Melbourne expanded in all directions in a land-consuming suburban sprawl. The city spread first to the east and north over the surrounding flat grasslands, and then southwards along the eastern shore of Port Phillip Bay. Wealthy new suburbs like South Yarra, Toorak, Kew and Malvern were laid out to accommodate elegant villas built on large blocks of land. The working classes settled on the other side of the Yarra River, in Richmond, Collingwood and Fitzroy, building cottages considered comfortable and roomy for the era. And it wasn't just private wealth that was growing; public infrastructure was expanding too. The new suburbs were serviced by networks of trains and trams that were among the largest and most modern in the world. Religious groups were given land to build schools, churches and cathedrals; the great civic institutions of Melbourne University

and the State Library of Victoria were founded.[18] All of this frenzied production needed materials: the houses needed framing, fittings and fences; the dancehalls needed floors; the churches needed altars and pews; the train lines needed sleepers; the schools, university and library needed desks and chairs and shelves; and everyone needed new coaches, travel luggage, furniture and all manner of consumer goods.[19] Suddenly, eyes turned to the forested hills which ringed the city, and before long a procession of timber-hauling bullock teams was treading the old Wurundjeri pathways up into the ranges, many of them stomping along the flatlands of Steels Creek en route.

The squatters and selectors had already taken all the land and most of the timber along the valley floor, but the steep slopes of the Great Dividing Range, all of which were Crown land, were the focus of the timber-getters from the start. From the top of the slopes, the horizon of dips and ridges that stretched into the distance, covered in massive and highly prized mountain ash, grey gum and the multipurpose stringybark, offered seemingly endless potential for profit in the booming Melbourne market. From as early as the 1870s, armed with not much more than their logging licence, a few rudimentary tools and often a young family, loggers made their camps on the slopes above the Steels Creek valley. This seasonal population was more animal than human, with bullocks outnumbering workers at the peak of summer by about 5 to 1. Bullock waggons carved a network of new tracks along the valley and across the slopes as they dragged their loads of split timber or whole tree trunks towards Melbourne. Timber-getting was hard work but not entirely unskilled. Felling the old giants was a dangerous job and it took a team of

17   Serle G (1977) *The Golden Age: A History of the Colony of Victoria, 1851–1861*. Melbourne University Press, Carlton.

18   Blainey G (2006) *A History of Victoria*. Cambridge University Press, Melbourne.

19   Davison G (2004) *The Rise and Fall of Marvellous Melbourne*. Melbourne University Press, Melbourne.

workers to bring down a tree safely. The trunk of the tree, once felled, was split into palings, with the longest and straightest trees producing about 12 000. An experienced splitter could produce a perfectly straight paling of even thickness with one stroke of the paling knife, and for a splitter at the top of his game, the money was not unattractive. Splitters were paid about 4 shillings a hundred for palings still in the forest but three times the price if they carted them to Melbourne. Easier said than done.[20]

For the timber-getters who worked in and around the valley, transport was a huge problem. The flood-prone Yarra Flats were a major obstacle in the winter, with bullock drays regularly being bogged to their axles. At certain times of the year work in the forests ceased altogether thanks to the impassable tracks and roads. If the requirements of Melbourne were to be satisfied, clearly some investment in substantial weatherproof infrastructure was required. What they needed was a railway.

Bullock train with hand-split palings.
(Provided by Rod Incoll, Forests Commission Retired Personnel Association)

Paling splitter at work.
(Provided by Rod Incoll, Forests Commission Retired Personnel Association)

20   Symonds S (1982) *Healesville: History in the Hills*. Pioneer Design Studio, Melbourne.

Trestle raised train line: an engineering feat.[21]

Thanks to astute lobbying from the local member, E.H. Cameron MLA, the Victorian Government agreed to fund a project on a scale the likes of which had not yet been seen in the colony. In a stunning feat of engineering, a railway line from Melbourne to Yarra Glen was built, lifted into the air on a series of 501 wooden trestles as it crossed the floodplain, forming a bridge that stretched a total of one and a half miles (3 km). Opened on 15 May 1888 this major new transport route allowed for economic opportunities of which the Yarra Valley timber entrepreneurs were quick to take advantage.[22] Even before the railway went through, steam powered mills had begun moving into the splitters' territory, producing higher grade timber products with their fine saws and accurate angles. But after the railway opened the number of timber mills exploded. At the peak of production there were upwards of a dozen timber mills centred around the Steels Creek area alone. The entire region, known as the Murrindindi forest area, included timber operations in Toolangi, Healesville and Yea and in its heyday was a mainstay of Victoria's economy. But with its economic wagon so closely hitched to the fortunes of Melbourne, the timber industry was in for a rough ride. Just a couple of years after the railway was opened, the big boom bubble that had floated 'marvellous Melbourne' for more than a generation burst in a spectacular crash, leaving behind a foaming economic wreck and a pile of unwanted timber sitting on the platform of the shiny new Yarra Glen railway station.

The bounce back from the crash was long and hard, and not just for timber workers; many thousands of people in Melbourne were suddenly and unexpectedly left in severely reduced circumstances. For the next couple of decades population growth stalled and investment froze. Of course firewood was always needed, no matter the economic circumstances, and the beautiful timbers of the Victorian forests were still in demand by those who could afford to build. But the good times were over, at least for the moment, and many of the millers whose saws had hummed across the ranges packed up shop and retreated into the valley to eke out a living as subsistence farmers.

* * *

For the thousands of people who found themselves unexpectedly out of work and out of money as the depression of 1891 hit, there was not much option but to spin the wheel of fortune and head back to the depleted goldfields.

---

21   Houghton N (1986) *Timber Mountain: A Sawmilling History of the Murrindindi Forest, 1885–1950*. Light Railway Research Society of Australia, Melbourne, p. 9.

22   Lee R, Annable R and Garden D (2007) *The Railways of Victoria 1854–2004*. Melbourne University Publishing, Melbourne.

Thanks to the new railway line to Yarra Glen, the previously poor-yielding fields of Steels Creek came into view as an attractive option. The place had been dug over during the main gold rush of the 1860s and a few small fortunes had been made – or so the rumours circulating in the city went. But once the easily panned gold had been sifted from the creeks, enthusiasm for the site dimmed. Thirty years later the rumours were back and almost overnight the northern end of the valley transformed into a city of tents and pits. By 1893 the local papers were reporting a crowd of several hundred men at the site, all of them digging, sluicing, drinking, fighting, striking it rich (rarely), and chasing a dream.[23]

Not all the miners had shipped in from the city. 'The Vagabond' reported in 1894 that a couple of local lads named Hunt had struck a promising reef which they named Lovie, not for any aspirations towards the theatre but after a fellow prospector who died suddenly without revealing the location of his rumoured 'rich vein'. Their neighbour William Bell resisted the temptation to sink a shaft himself, but happily leased low-lying sections of his land to others to try their luck. Ever the businessman though, Bell was happy to provide butter, vegetables and other fresh supplies to the diggers and reputedly made a nice profit. The crowd of hungry young men and their gold dust soon attracted the attention of other entrepreneurs and something as close to a village as Steels Creek has ever seen began to take shape. An ironmonger, a general store and a pub sprang up and the butcher from Yarra Glen began regular deliveries to the tents. One creative entrepreneur even started a sightseeing venture, leading parties of Melbournians along the valley floor to visit the mines. A ride on a steam train to Yarra Glen, a buggy ride around the diggings, a picnic in the bush

and a return to the warmth of the pub for dinner was a perfect weekend outing for well-heeled city folk and, with a little help from the press, the trend took off.

By the turn of the century the gold rush had fizzled out without ever really having fired up. The shops shut and the miners moved on. All that was left were the shafts. But, not surprisingly, the tourists kept coming. If it was a trip to the diggings that inspired the early visits to the valley, it was the natural beauty of the place that called people back. The magnificent forests of giant trees and gullies of lush tree ferns proved a massive draw and coaches were soon lining up to ferry visitors from the train terminus in Yarra Glen along Steels Creek Road, the main route through to the tall forests. What began as a sideline to the diggings soon became one of the most important strands in the local economy: the day of the grand guesthouse had dawned. By the 1920s the upper Yarra Valley was accommodating between 5000 and 6000 visitors at the height of the holiday season.[24]

As more and more people were exposed to the beauty of 'big nature' in the Yarra Ranges, so more and more of them became advocates for its protection. By the 1920s timber workers had severely depleted stocks of timber from the easily accessible areas of forest and the remnant bush was increasingly being cleared for agriculture. The vistas of tall trees and lush ferns were disappearing at an alarming rate. But the bush had its champions. In a move that would set the scene for conflicts over land use for the next century, a group of concerned individuals formed a lobby group to advocate for the protection of at least part of the Yarra Ranges forests in perpetuity. Among the group

23   Tetlow E (2005) *Recollections and Records of Mining at Steels Creek, Victoria*. Yarra Glen and District Historical Society, Publication Series no. 1.

24   Symonds S (1982) *Healesville: History in the Hills*. Pioneer Design Studio, Melbourne.

Greenwood Guesthouse, circa 1930s (Courtesy of Yarra Glen & District Historical Society). The fine Edwardian timber building that was once the Greenwood guesthouse snuggles into a shoulder of rock above the road at the most northerly end of the Steels Creek valley. It is the sole survivor of its type, having seen off more fires than any other building at this end of the valley. You can tell from the size of the verandahs and the pitch of the roof that this elegant old home has been the scene of many a fine afternoon tea. Perhaps it was to encourage the appetite of his guests that its original owner, Mr Giddens, cut a walking track from the back of the house to the top of Mt Slide. The track wove up through the stands of massive tree ferns in the gully into the tall forests of the Great Dividing Range. High above the valley floor, where the manna gum and messmate forest gives over to mountain grey gum and mountain ash, the tourists could stop for a picnic and have a round of their favourite game, linking arms to measure the girth of the ancient giants. Eight man trees, six man trees, nine man trees, their crowns stretching so far into the sky as to be almost beyond sight.

Tree hugging, 1910, in what would become the Kinglake National Park.[25]

25   St Andrews Primary School Council (1998) *St Andrews: A Village Built on Gold.* St Andrews, Victoria, p. 15.

was William Laver, Professor of Music at Melbourne University and owner of a property in Jehosaphat Gully, adjacent to Steels Creek Road. Seeking to set an example, the Professor donated his own 23 hectares to the cause. In 1928, 5590 hectares of forest were formally reserved to be managed by a committee for the Lands Department.[26] The Kinglake National Park was born. Why it was named after English author and lawyer Alexander W. Kinglake, famous in his day for a massive eight-volume history of the Crimean War (but not for having visited Australia even once in his lifetime), is no longer known. However, sitting as it does on the outskirts of Melbourne, it is the best known and, some would say, the most loved in the Yarra Ranges region.[27]

Today the buzz of light aircraft from the nearby aerodrome provides a background soundtrack to weekends in Steels Creek as tourists follow the contours of the escarpment and the Dividing Range from the air. If you fancy extending your stay, a range of bed and breakfast accommodation is available, starting with the bunk beds at the organic farm through to five star cabins in lush garden settings. On the ground, the roads of the Steels Creek valley still hum with tourists; the Mt Slide Road is used for the annual Ford car rally, Steels Creek Road for bicycle races in the warmer months and the fire tracks of the Kinglake National Park for bushwalking, horse riding and mountain biking all year round.[28] Melbourne is still in love with the 'big nature' on its fringe.

* * *

While mining, timber and tourism were developing in the foreground of the Steels Creek economy, the real story behind the scenes was land acquisition. In 1856 a new land owning scheme was introduced that offered 'probationary leases' to prospective farmers. A 'selector' could choose between 40 and 640 acres that they could then rent from the government for 2 shillings per acre, per year. If the land was 'improved' – through draining, clearing, fencing, building a house, running livestock or growing crops – to the value of one pound per acre, at the end of one year the selector could either buy the property outright or continue to lease it for another seven years, after which it would be theirs to own freehold. When this scheme became law in the middle of 1865 it was an instant hit. Some of the newly opened Land Officers were flooded with up to 3000 applicants a day.[29]

This Amending Land Act of 1865 gave the Yarra Valley farming community its breath of life. In the Burgoyne Parish alone 46 selectors are listed as having taken up the offer.[30] This group, all of them Anglo-Celtic in origin, introduced a new social order into the valley. While the land was cleared, fenced and grazed, the families who worked these selections began to form the structures that would shape both the land and the community for generations into the future. The Campbells, the Donaldsons, the Hargreaves, the Hubbards, the Hunts, the Jewsons, the Johnstons, the Littles, the Scotts, the Williamsons: this rollcall of early families is the backbone of Steels Creek social history. Far from watching the ebb and flow of the mining, timber and tourist industries, they

26   Garnet JR and Victorian National Parks Association (1958) *Kinglake National Park*. Victorian National Parks Association, Melbourne.
27   Tuckwell W (1902) *A.W. Kinglake. 1829–1919*. G. Bell & Sons, London.
28   Williams A (1996) *Steels Creek: Vineyards, Landscape and Development*. University of Melbourne, Melbourne, pp. 28–9.
29   Lewis W, Balderstone S and Bowan J (2006) *Events That Shaped Australia*. New Holland, Sydney.
30   List of early landowners courtesy of the Yarra Glen and District Historical Society.

were often the main instigators. From sawmills, to mine shafts, to guesthouses, to orchards, these enterprising dynasties worked every angle, often with much success. One celebratory local history reports that:

> *When [William] Hubbard settled on his farm [of 320 acres in 1865,] the place was little else than a wilderness, but after he cleared, drained and fenced it, the property was one of the finest in the district. He was awarded a bronze medal and also a diploma at the Amsterdam Exhibition in 1883 for an exhibit of corn. He took no fewer than thirteen first prizes for the best exhibit of oats at the Victorian Agricultural Society's shows at Heidelberg.[31]*

This Hubbard, formerly of Norfolk, England, could not have guessed that his grandson, Gordon Hubbard, would one day be the star of the Steels Creek cricket club, sawmill operator, rescuer of women and children from bushfire, generous employer of local labour and all-round home-grown local hero.

By the 1890s many of the larger farms were being subdivided into smaller lots and the job of transforming the Steels Creek landscape, begun by the selectors, was completed: acres of timber were cleared, miles of fences were erected, billabongs and marshes were drained and a network of roads and tracks were laid. As the 20th century rolled around, the era of the small acreage subsistence farmer had arrived. Without the land needed for farming on a scale that could make a profit, yet tied to the vicissitudes of the local economy, this generation (many of them descendants of selectors) struggled and scraped through the turbulent decades that followed. As everywhere else in Australia at the time, cars were rare, money was tight and ingenuity was highly prized. This era of community, still extant in local oral histories, set the tone of valley life into the future: funny, inventive, irreverent, observant, occasionally athletic and often not a little eccentric, the Steels Creek 'local' came into being. It was no doubt this fusion of battler and dreamer that inspired the contemporary community to take their obligation as inheritors of the 'Screekian' cultural lineage seriously.

* * *

If Steels Creek is, as Keith Montell proposes, a 'state of mind', then it's a state of mind worth preserving. And perhaps it was this state of mind, as much as the physical location, that was threatened by the bushfires of 2009. Although the charm of the place is its refusal to be obvious, in times of trouble the lack of physical definition has its downside. With the eruption of commentary, reportage, enquiries and publicity that followed the Black Saturday disaster, Steels Creek barely rated a mention. Yet for the small community, the consequences of the fires were shattering. In the weeks following 7 February 2009, 10 memorials were held for friends and family members who perished in the fires. More than 70 per cent of the housing stock was demolished along with all contents, leaving the families who lived in those properties homeless. Children lost pets, adults lost confidence. But still, at the end of it all, the people of Steels Creek had each other.

---

31   Blackburn GL (1968) *A History of the Yarra Glen District, developed and published for the Yarra Glen State School Centenary Celebrations*. Yarra Glen State School Centenary Celebrations Committee, Yarra Glen.

As the blackened ridge lines above the valley are subsumed by the emerging forest, the story of Black Saturday will dim and become another layer of history, remembered by some but never heard of by others. The population of this valley will shift again as the suburbs of Melbourne grow ever closer. The stories of the 2009 fire will persist for a while, but as generational and demographic change churns through the local population, the story will fade into 'the past'. If it is another 70 years before the next great storm of fire bursts out of the ranges, what reminders are we leaving that will help the next generation to survive? How do we sow the history of our generation into the layered soil of what has come before?

Mud-map of the Steels Creek valley by Malcolm Calder.

Our place

Views of the valley

The pictures on the following pages introduce the natural and farming worlds of Steels Creek – the bush, the land and the way we live in a country community in Australia. Included are some of the activities that are based in our Community Centre, which was previously the Steels Creek Primary School.

The Community Centre acts as the focal point for anyone who lives in Steels Creek, although not everyone chooses to be involved. The centre is host to community and local events as well as activity groups such as the Garden Club, SC Stitchers, SC Art Group, the SC Clamberers, Friday Night Films, the SC Book Group, SC Landcare and the Saturday Market.

The productive landscape of Steels Creek in December 2008. This view (below left) is looking south from Pinnacle Lane towards what was Roundstone Vineyards and Restaurant. There are vineyards, grazing pasture and hay in a basin surrounded by native bush. Following the Black Saturday fires, the only remaining structure at Roundstone was the pizza oven within a tangled mass of mortar and steel.

What a difference a day makes! Steels Creek landscape on 12 February 2009 (below right), looking west across the valley from Pinnacle Lane. Now the view is of a bruised and battered landscape surrounded by hills outlined in 'black lace'.

Looking up

Country conversations often include comments on the weather, the jobs to be done, maybe helping a neighbour or planning a project. The sky and the landscape provide vital signs of the weather and the conditions that may influence your day and your plans.

The clouds have much to say on current and future weather, and there are also the humans up there in aeroplanes, helicopters, ultra-lites and hot air balloons. In the photographs below the messages are: the summer shower has passed (top left); continuing fine weather (middle top); there is a storm coming in from the north-west (bottom left); clear weather is on its way (bottom middle); and sometimes the skies have a more sinister message, as on Black Saturday (below right). In late summer, flights of white-throated needletails often pass over ahead of the cold front (above).

White-throated needletails by Margaret McLoughlin.

Looking down

The ground at our feet also offers us clues. Blackbird nest (top left); forest fungi (left); Hardenbergia seedling (below left) and fire moss (bottom left). Every farm dam has its population of yabbies (centre). Black-fronted dotterells at their nest on a driveway (right), and the cracked earth of a dam in drought (bottom right).

Our valley

Steels Creek runs from north to south from the Kinglake slopes of the Great Divide. Its headwaters are in the tall ash forests of Kinglake National Park. Along the centre of the wide valley floor, the Creek – due to former 'river improvement' works – runs in a deeply eroded channel and its banks are tunnelled with the burrows of wasps and wombats. However, looking from Steels Creek Road, there is the beauty of the stately, white-trunked manna gums and in spring a golden thread of wattles runs through the length of the valley. After the Black Saturday fire, a scarred landscape recovers.

Living in the landscape

The community of Steels Creek covers the full range of households including young families with parents working away from home, families who make their living in the valley as primary producers or work in the burgeoning tourist industry, commuters and retirees. Since the 1970s the community has expanded to include couples on bush blocks, retirees, those wanting a more rural life style and people with part-time smallholdings. The joy of living in the country is a driving force behind the community.

The Steels Creek walking group ('The Clamberers') exploring the local bush.

Land and life in Steels Creek: farming (top left); gardening in the valley and the Garden Club Flower Show and evening barbecue (lower left); the Garden Club propagating group at work (top right); and the Stitchers put the final touches to their fire-recovery Phoenix Quilt (lower right). The quilt is also pictured at the end of this book, on the inside back cover.

Three stories

Albie and Gwen Leckie – the farmers

Since the earliest days of European settlement, the Steels Creek valley has been involved in farming and rural production. Over the years, as timber milling has given way to vineyards, the grazing of cattle has continued.

Continuing this tradition, Albie and Gwen Leckie have successfully run a herd of beef cattle for over 30 years at the top end of Steels Creek valley. On 7 February 2009, they reluctantly evacuated at the height of the fires. Albie and his son returned early the next morning, unsure of what might remain of the house and farm. Armed with a rifle, Albie was prepared for the worst. Despite the devastation all around with smouldering trees and fence posts, and sheds and cattle-yards reduced to heaps of twisted metal, Albie was amazed to find his home still standing and unburnt. And clustered around the scorched, but intact, hay shed were all his cattle ready for a morning round of hay!

The years following Black Saturday have brought challenges of personal recovery and the physical demands of rebuilding and restoring sheds, fences and yards – as well as the traumatised community of Steels Creek. Albie and Gwen have played a central part in this, providing support and encouragement to many friends and families in the valley. At the same time they have continued to operate their farm and lives together. It has been a massive task for them at a time when most expect to be enjoying the quieter life of semi-retirement.

Tony and Georgina Woolley – the animal carers

Tony and Georgina are devoted to the welfare of wildlife, and for a number of years before Black Saturday ran an animal shelter at the top end of Steels Creek Road.

Life as an animal carer is a major commitment of time and resources. It means being 'open for business' at all hours and involves the care and security of sick and injured animals and being always ready to welcome the next patient. On average there are around 70 or so animals in residence at any one time. The daily routine requires checking each animal in pens, sheds or cages and making sure that all structures are proofed against predators or escape. Access to water is essential for each animal. The feeding routine starts around 6 am with the preparation of each specialised diet; the seven wombats currently in care eat through 7 kg of sweet potato each week. Feeding continues through the day and into the evening, often going on to 9 pm. There are two feeding rounds each day, seven days a week, 52 weeks a year.

On Black Saturday Tony and Georgina lost the entire operation – sheds, pens, food stores and their house. There was nothing left but a twisted, smouldering mass of timber and iron. The couple were lucky to escape with their lives. On the days following the fires, when the need for care of injured animals was most acute, they had no capacity to provide help. All Tony could do was to accompany the vet from Healesville Sanctuary as they attended to injured animals, many of which had to be destroyed, so far were they beyond recovery.

Now the couple run a new animal shelter in neighbouring Dixons Creek on land generously donated by a local landholder, and the busy round of caring for native animals continues.

Jenny and John Barnett – the naturalists

Jenny and John were both born in England and came to love the Australian bush. They spent their weekends in their house at the top end of Old Kinglake Road bordering the Kinglake National Park. It was set in the dry woodland forest of the Christmas Hills ridge. Both Jenny and John were trained biologists and had professional employment in Melbourne. Jenny (née Forse) completed an MSc on native ants and also developed a passion for the biology and cultivation of orchids. She was conducting an ongoing study of the ground orchids on their property since the fires of 1992. Jenny was actively involved in many of the conservation campaigns of the Victorian National Parks Association, served on the VNPA Council and was Vice-President from 1988 to 1993. At the time of her death she was working on a study of the impact of fire on different environments to assist better planning for both human safety and conservation. In the 1980s and 1990s, together with Rosemary Baker, she developed the 'bible' on local conservation called *Standing Up for Your Local Environment: An Action Guide*. John was a distinguished mammalogist, completed a PhD on Australian mammals and stress physiology, and had an international scientific reputation through his work over many decades in animal welfare. His research and advocacy led to great improvements in animal husbandry techniques for farmed animals, especially pigs and poultry.

Jenny and John were keen bushwalkers and came on many of the walks organised by the Community Centre. In spring, a highlight for our Clamberers Group was Jenny's annual orchid walk when she shared both her knowledge and love of the many beautiful, but overlooked local native orchids.

Although their house was designed to be bush-fire resistant and they chose to stay and defend, the fire of 7 February unfortunately came with such speed and force that they had no hope. Along with eight other people in Steels Creek they lost their lives on Black Saturday.

Bush

Tom Griffiths

The horseshoe of hills surrounding Steels Creek – known to Aboriginal people as *Wyenondable*, the Fiery Hills – includes vast tracts of state forest and national park. On Black Saturday, as the firestorm surged from the north-west towards Steels Creek, the tall trees in the Mount Disappointment and Humevale forests threw flaming firebrands before the wind. Burning streamers of bark were carried over 30 km ahead of the fire front and, in the words of Colleen Keating watching from the Kangaroo Ground fire tower, exploded 'like a bomb being dropped' into Strathewen, St Andrews and the Steels Creek valley. Those trees had, in a sense, been waiting for exactly that day, and they were fulfilling their destiny.

Trees of the fire flume

Fire is the key force that has shaped the bush. The first human settlers of Australia were possibly lured to the continent by smoke. About 55 000 years ago, the first long-distance sea voyagers in the history of humanity gazed out from South-East Asia towards a blue, oceanic horizon. How did they guess there might be land over the rim of the sea? Perhaps they watched the glow of distant fires in the night sky or in daylight saw distant smoke from the burning bush.

The Australia that awaited these most adventurous of all humans was already a continent of fire. Once part of a southern Gondwanan supercontinent dominated by rainforest, the Australian fragment broke away 45 million years ago and rafted northwards into warmer, drier latitudes, 7 centimetres a year. Antarctica remained at the pole and became isolated and refrigerated by a strengthening circumpolar current. As an ice cap formed at the South Pole – one that would grow several kilometres high – the Earth became cooler and drier. Australia journeyed to lower latitudes and became a different sort of desert, one shaped by fire.

The continent began to leach, dry and burn. Australia's ancient soils became degraded and impoverished and were hardly renewed or disturbed by glaciers or volcanoes. The land became more arid and the inland seas began to dry up. The subtropical high-pressure systems of the latitudes of the 'thirsty thirties' controlled the new weather. Fire became more frequent and dominant. Under the combined assault of soil degradation, aridity and fire, the greenery of Gondwana burnished into a different kind of vegetation. Hard-leaved, sclerophyll plants emerged from within the rainforest to dominate and diversify, eucalypts dramatically extended their range, casuarinas succeeded araucarias, and grasses flourished and largely replaced the dominant rainforest species. Ferns, moss and fungi still persist in the shelter of bush canopies.[1]

Ferns along Greenwood Lane.

The arrival of humans with their firesticks further fostered flame and strengthened the reign of the eucalypt.[2] Fire is at the very heart of Aboriginal civilisation, as it is of the nature of Australia. Just as the first Aboriginal colonisers of Australia had probably observed the distant smoke of the burning continent, so did European voyagers also find a 'continent of smoke', as Captain James Cook called it.[3] This time the smoke indicated human presence, and the Europeans saw the smoke of Aboriginal fires before they met the people. Coastal smoke signals seemed to presage the progress of the

1   Pyne SJ (1992) *Burning Bush: A Fire History of Australia*. Allen & Unwin, Sydney, 'Prologue'; White ME (1986) *The Greening of Gondwana*. Reed Books, Sydney; and Rolls E (1997) The nature of Australia. In: *Ecology and Empire: Environmental History of Settler Societies*. (Eds T Griffiths and L Robin) pp. 35–45. Keele University Press, Edinburgh.

2   There is an important debate about the impact of Aboriginal landscape burning on the Australian biota, a discussion ably reviewed by David Bowman (1998) in 'Tansley Review no. 101: the impact of Aboriginal landscape burning on the Australian biota', *New Phytologist* **140**, 385–410. See also Gammage B (2011) *The Biggest Estate on Earth: How Aborigines Made Australia*. Allen & Unwin, Sydney.

3   Quoted in Pyne SJ, *Burning Bush*, p. 136.

explorers' ships, and even when the sailors went ashore they found smoke trails and abandoned campfires more easily than the wary residents. When the European voyagers did encounter the Australians, the locals were carrying firesticks. Aboriginal people cooked, farmed, fought and celebrated with fire. 'The natives were about, burning, burning, ever burning; one would think they were of the fabled salamander race, and lived on fire instead of water', wrote explorer Ernest Giles in 1889.[4]

The landscape was, as the European colonists kept saying, like a 'gentleman's park': it was mostly lightly treed, open country. Historian Bill Gammage has observed that the second most common word in colonial descriptions of landscape after 'bush' was 'park'. The term 'park' had its origins in 12th-century Britain as a description of aristocratic reserves for hunting, and colonists enjoyed riding their horses through an open landscape: 'If a kangaroo or an emu should start up in your path, you enjoy a clear and animated view of the chase, until the dogs finally surround and seize upon their victim', wrote Peter Cunningham, a pastoralist on the Upper Hunter River of NSW.

In appreciating this open terrain, settlers sometimes wondered at their good fortune. The visiting writer William Howitt commented on the 'most civilised look' of the landscape: 'You would have said it was a cultivated sheep farming country, like Wiltshire, but it was as nature had left it.'[5] Charles Griffith described the plains west of Melbourne in 1845 in similar terms: 'That which

from my first arrival has always struck me as the main characteristic of the country is, its remarkably civilised appearance. It is difficult … not to fancy that the hand of man had been engaged in combing and arranging the elements of natural beauty.'[6] And, of course, it had.

As the anthropologist Sylvia Hallam put it in her book, *Fire and Hearth*, the land that the settlers thought they had discovered was 'not as God made it. It was as the Aborigines made it.'[7] On the wooded plains and the margins of the wet sclerophyll forests Aboriginal people kept their hunting grounds open and freshly grassed by light regular burning. By burning small patches at a time, they controlled large wildfires and encouraged an abundance of medium-sized mammals. Another anthropologist, Rhys Jones, called this 'fire-stick farming', a phrase that cleverly challenged the widespread settler's prejudice that Aborigines were not farmers and therefore did not manage or own land.[8] Farming with the firestick created open woodlands of mature, well-spaced trees, and fostered the dominance of grass species. Today, Australians are still slow to recognise the complexity and intentionality of Indigenous fire practices. Tens of thousands of years of systematic Aboriginal burning had cultivated a squatter's dream.

Thus 'The Bush', often granted a capital 'B' and so much a part of Australia's distinctive identity, has a complex natural and human history. It was a product of geological forces – the breaking up of old Gondwana and the

4   Giles E (1889) *Australia Twice Traversed: The Romance of Exploration*. Sampson Low, Marston, Searle & Rivington, London, p. 81.

5   Barr N and Cary J (1992) *Greening a Brown Land: The Australian Search for Sustainable Land Use*. Macmillan Education Australia, Melbourne, pp. 6–7.

6   Griffith C (1845) *The present state and prospects of the Port Phillip District of New South Wales*. William Curry Jun. & Co., Dublin, pp. 7–8.

7   Hallam S (1979) *Fire and Hearth: A Study of Aboriginal Usage and European Usurpation in Southeastern Australia*. Australian Institute of Aboriginal Studies, Canberra, p. vii.

8   Jones R (1969) Fire-stick farming. *Australian Natural History* **16**, 224–228.

impoverishment of soils that accompanied the journey of the Australian fragment into drier latitudes. It was a product of biological history – the retreat of the rainforest to clefts and gullies as fire became a dominant ecological agent and the eucalypt asserted its reign. It was a product of ancient human civilisation – the constant burning of vegetation by the first Australians and the creation of hunting grounds through firestick farming. It was a product of European colonisation – the imperial urge to 'improve' the land by clearing trees and scrub for stock and crops and the creation of reserves for useful timber. 'The Bush' that we know today was shaped by all these forces, and the forested river flats and foothills that became Steels Creek were made and re-made by them.

To appreciate the Australian bush in all its beauty and dangerous power, we need to see it as historical – as a dynamic evolving biological force with regenerative purpose in the midst of which humans have the craving and courage to live. And we need to see 'The Bush', sometimes portrayed as an amorphous olive-green mantle, as actually a tapestry of diverse communities each with distinctive histories, and each with a different ecology of fire. This was hard for some European colonists and their descendants to perceive, for their senses were schooled to a different aesthetic. Many nostalgic British settlers thought Australian birds songless and they condemned the gum forests as monotonous. Yet there are hundreds of varieties of eucalypt, and each individual of the same species looks different. Each gum tree grows and branches differently and its pendulous leaves display a trunk and boughs with unique colour, personality and character. The eucalypt forest is a community

of raffish individuals. Just as Australians have come to learn that their birds are among the most extravagantly musical in the world, so they have come to see the ubiquitous gum forests as surprisingly varied and beautiful. They are flamboyant, combustible wooden sculpture parks.

What kind of trees and what kind of fire do the residents of Steels Creek live with? On a planet wrought by fire there is the fire continent of Australia, and in Australia there is a fire region that is the most dangerous in the world, and in that distinctive region is Steels Creek. Victorians live within what the international fire historian Stephen Pyne calls 'the fire flume'.[9] When a high-pressure system stalls in the Tasman Sea, hot northerly winds flow relentlessly down from central Australia across the densely vegetated south-east of the continent. This fiery 'flume' brews a deadly chemistry of air and fuel. The mountain topography of steep slopes, ridges and valleys accelerates and channels the hot air, temperatures climb to searing extremes in January and February, and humidity evaporates such that the air crackles. Lightning attacks the land ahead of the delayed cold front and a dramatic southerly change can turn a raging fire suddenly upon its victims.

There is a further ingredient to the chemistry of the fire flume. In the forests of the Victorian and Tasmanian ranges, a distinctive type of eucalypt has evolved. As you climb from the Steels Creek valley up the ridges surrounding it and beyond, the manna gums (*Eucalyptus viminalis*) that cluster along the creek and the messmate stringybark (*E. obliqua*), yellow box (*E. melliodora*) and brown stringybark (*E. baxteri*) of the flats and lower slopes give way to taller,

---

9   Pyne SJ, *Burning Bush*, 1992.

*Mountain grey gum (*E. cypellocarpa*) on Greenwood Lane, fire-scarred on Black Saturday.*

wetter forests of narrow-leaved peppermint (*E. radiata*), silvertop (*E. sieberi*) and mountain grey gum (*E. cypellocarpa*) – and, if you keep going, you eventually reach towering stands of mountain ash (*E. regnans*). The mountain ash was described by the botanist who pioneered its study, David Ashton, as 'the supreme expression of the genus *Eucalyptus*'.[10] It is a tree of wonder, the tallest flowering plant in the world.

Eucalyptus regnans – which means 'ruling' or 'reigning' – grows to 100 metres and lives for centuries. Colonists cut it down to measure its height. The trunk of the mountain ash is a smooth white or greenish grey and it sheds long ribbons of bark. At its base clings a rough fibrous stocking. It is a very rapid grower and can reach a height of 40 metres in 20 years. The mountain ash is consequently more slender than one would expect for its height, and its crown looks disproportionately small (for a forest giant) and is rather open with pendant leaves. It dominates the wet sclerophyll forest of the Yarra Ranges and generally occurs in pure, even-aged stands, each of which was seeded in a massive crown fire. At its feet, among the heavy leaf litter, there move puny people whose lifetimes are a sixth of that of the trees. Here is the fatal mismatch between the biographies of the people and the biographies of the trees they aspire to manage.

10   Ashton DH (1981) Tall-open forest. In: *Australian Vegetation*. (Ed. RH Groves) pp. 121–151. Cambridge University Press, Cambridge.

Mature mountain ash forest in the Wallaby Creek catchment area, Mount Disappointment, in 1992.

Ash-type eucalypts (the mountain and alpine ash) have developed a different means of regeneration. Although they may occasionally produce epicormic shoots from their branches after fire, drought or insect damage, they do not develop lignotubers under the ground from which they can renew themselves, and mountain ash and alpine ash rarely coppice (that is, grow new shoots from a cut stump). For their survival, therefore, they are unusually dependent on their seed supply. Mountain ash dies out unless fire periodically sweeps the forest, for it is principally fire that releases the seed from the tree's hard capsules. However, the tree is also unusually sensitive to fire. Its bark is thin, and mature trees are easily killed by fire. Mountain ash grows in the high rainfall areas on the southern slopes of the Divide where it is protected from desiccating northerly winds. Fire generally intrudes only after several years of drought and on very hot windy days, but when it does intrude it rages high and far.[11]

If no firestorm sweeps the forest during the 400-year lifetime of mountain ash, the ash forest dies out. Sometimes beneath the tall mountain-ash canopy a fully developed rainforest of myrtle beech and southern sassafras bides its time, ready to become dominant in the long absence of fire, ready to reassert its ancestral priority. If fire sweeps the forest too frequently – at intervals of less than 15 or 20 years, as has happened since European settlement in some places – the young ash does not have time to produce seed and again the ash forest dies, replaced this time by bracken, silver wattle (*Acacia dealbata*) and scrub. It is a precarious balance, and thus these tall, noble eucalypts may be described as 'transient fire weeds'.[12] Aboriginal people would have known of their deadly character and avoided the forests in high summer, while in other seasons they ventured into them in search of lyrebird tails and the edible hearts of tree ferns.

So these great forests of ash renew themselves *en masse*. These magnificent trees have evolved to commit mass suicide. There are no saplings in a mature mountain ash forest, for the seedlings need the light that floods in when the entire canopy is removed, and they thrive in a soil stocked with post-fire nutrients, free of fungus, and with a reduced

11   Ashton D (1956) Studies on the autecology of *Eucalyptus regnans* F.v.M. PhD thesis, School of Botany, University of Melbourne; and Ashton D (1981) Fire in tall open-forests (wet sclerophyll forests). In: *Fire and the Australian Biota*. (Eds AM Gill, RH Groves and IR Noble) pp. 339–366. Australian Academy of Science, Canberra. See also Galbraith AV (1937) *Mountain Ash: A General Treatise on Its Silviculture, Management and Utilisation*. Forests Commission of Victoria, Melbourne.

12   Cremer KW (1960) Eucalypts in rain forest. *Australian Forestry* **24**, 120–126, quoted in Bowman DMJS (2000) *Australian Rainforests: Islands of Green in a Land of Fire*. Cambridge University Press, Cambridge, p. 268.

population of insects. The mountain ash forests are therefore adapted to, and a product of, intense crown fires that occurred once every few hundred years. Not all the communities that were incinerated in 2009 were in or near the forests of ash, but many were, and the peculiar fire ecology of the trees is another deadly dimension of this distinctive fire environment. These are wet mountain forests that only burn on rare days at the end of long droughts, after prolonged heatwaves, and when the flume is in full gear. And when they do burn, they do so with atomic power.

One of those tall trees that combusted near Mount Disappointment and Humevale on Black Saturday and hurled its flaming firebrands of bark into the wind towards Steels Creek was an elegant and healthy giant called 'Mr Jessop'. It was named by the botanist David Ashton after the Chairman of the Melbourne and Metropolitan Board of Works, John Jessop (1892–1968) for his role in encouraging old growth forest research in the post-war period. At over 90 metres in height and almost 9 metres in girth, 'Mr Jessop' was, on the eve of Black Saturday, one of the contenders for the title of tallest living tree in Victoria. Over 300 years old, it lived in a cathedral of a forest known as the Big Ash in the Wallaby Creek catchment next to the Kinglake National Park. On 7 February 2009, when the Kilmore East fire surged south-eastwards across the Hume Highway and entered these forests, the fire's behaviour changed. The wind shifted slightly so that it bore directly upon the facing slopes of Mount Disappointment. In the words of CFA Senior Wildfire Instructor, Fabian Crowe, 'the slopes of Mount Disappointment were welcoming the fire'. 'Mr Jessop' and his kin were welcoming it too.

'Mr Jessop', a mountain ash (E. regnans) on Mount Disappointment, 1992.

David Ashton and Mr Jessop in 1992.

Thanks to his brilliant ecological research after the 1939 fires and the Second World War, David Ashton (one of Malcolm Calder's colleagues in the Melbourne University Botany School) was able to elucidate the apparently paradoxical relationship between mountain ash and fire. He found that it created 'a miracle of timing'.[13] Mountain ash is very sensitive to light surface fires, but seeds prolifically in intense crown fires. In fact it possesses features that seem to promote such fires: a heavy fall of highly flammable leaf litter (two or three times that of other eucalypts) particularly in dry seasons, hanging streamers of bark that take the flames up to the canopy and become those firebrands propelled by the wind in advance of the flame, and open crowns whose pendulous foliage encourages updrafts. And how do these precious seeds survive the intense heat that they indubitably need? Ashton suggests that perhaps it is the very flammability of the crown that protects the seed in its capsule – just long enough. In the crown of the tree ahead of the fire front, the heat is brief and explosive and, some observers say, is followed by cool updrafts of air before the arrival of the surface fire. This fragile and complex circumstance certainly works. At Noojee after the 1939 fires, forester A.H. Beetham found that nearly 2.5 million seedlings per hectare of mountain ash germinated.[14] The conditions that create a 'miracle of timing' for this tall eucalypt are the very same ones that conjure a firestorm from hell for any humans in its path. Black Saturday was typical of this region.

Thus the mountain ash forests defy some of the ecological and historical generalisations about Australian forests, especially those that apply to the continent's ubiquitous dry woodlands. The forests of ash, by contrast to the drier forests, have little resistance to fire. Their regeneration is precarious. They were not burnt lightly and regularly by Aborigines. Firestorms are endemic. The very existence of mature ash forests, such as those inhabited by 'Mr Jessop', is testimony to a finely balanced fire regime of very occasional widespread and intense conflagrations.[15]

One of the most celebrated sawmillers of the mountain ash, Hec Ingram, fondly called it a 'parochial timber'.[16] And within its restricted domain and influence sits Steels Creek – and Kinglake, Marysville, Flowerdale, Strathewen, St Andrews and many other human communities blitzed on Black Saturday. Standing tall in noble ranks on the ridges above and beyond the Steels Creek valley is this extraordinary giant, ready to sacrifice itself and every one of its kind for the future of the forest. In the mixed, drier forest below, the other eucalypts congregate, like servants to their king. They feed him fire, and feed off his fire. When he falls – when the kingdom falls – they fall.

13   Ashton, 'Fire in tall open-forests', p. 362.
14   Beetham AH (1950) Aspects of forest practice in the regenerated areas of the upper Latrobe Valley. Diploma of Forestry thesis, Department of Primary Industries Library, Victoria.
15   Ashton, 'Fire in tall open-forests'.
16   Ingram H (1979) *Early Forest Utilisation*. Forest Recollections series, Institute of Foresters of Australia, Victorian Division, Mitcham, p. 6.

Life among the stringybark

'Bush' is a potent four-letter word. Few other words so powerfully distil the essence of Australia. A sprig of wattle sent to a homesick traveller, the scent of eucalyptus inhaled on the sea air by a returning voyager and the smoky-blue haze of a mountain horizon all conjure the bush. As the *Australian National Dictionary* reveals with its chronological mapping of language, changing usage of the word 'bush' provides a mini environmental history of Australia. This punchy word can generalise vast tracts of land or describe quite specific kinds of country.[17]

In 1834, John Dunmore Lang explained that 'the word bush … sometimes signifies the country in general, but more properly the uncleared part of it'. So he was saying, first of all, that The Bush was not The City. Thus 'Sydney or The Bush' became a famous dichotomy in the history of New South Wales. As the *Sydney Herald* put it in 1841, when you are in the bush, you are 'beyond the region of civilization'. Often, however, the bush embraced everything beyond the city, including country towns. As the visiting English author Anthony Trollope put it in 1873: 'Instead of a town mouse and a country mouse in Australia, there would be a town mouse and a bush mouse – but mice living in small country towns would still be bush mice.'

But Lang also defined 'bush' in the more specific sense of uncleared land. This was a common meaning. As one observer of Australian life explained in 1960, 'Anything smaller than a river is a creek, anything not flat is a gully, any piece of land is a paddock, any vegetation is bush.' Bush, it was declared in 1851,

was 'the colonial name for all kinds of wild vegetation'. One traveller in 1836 explained that, 'Our road lay through the *bush*. In India, I should have said the *jungle*, and in Europe, the *forest*. The bush is a generic term in the colony, and signifies a district of the country in a state of nature.'

This definition of bush as land 'in a state of nature' left open the surprising possibility that bush could be open country. It could be 'uncleared' yet also free of vegetation. Bush was 'wilderness'; it was a tract of country 'in a state of nature, uncultivated and unenclosed'. The word here becomes caught up in the colonial politics of land. 'Bush', by generalising open and forested land, paid no attention to the complex mosaic of vegetation created by Aboriginal firestick farming, and therefore made the dispossession of Aboriginal people less visible. And secondly, there was also an implication that mere pastoralism was insufficient for the transformation of bush. *An Emigrant's Guide* of 1849 explained that bush was 'wild and unreclaimed country, in which the sheep and cattle farmers are mere squatters on the soil'. By contrast, it was agriculture (or 'enclosure') that would properly turn bush into civilisation. Bush might even be a transitional state itself: in 1953 one writer identified bush as 'the Australian word for the newly-settled country even when there is not a bush upon it'.

The word 'bush' could also describe particular types of vegetation. In 1873, Trollope explained that bush was passable on horseback, whereas 'scrub' was not. Another writer in 1840 recorded that bush 'may be most truly described as the very reverse of the "more thickly wooded part of the country"'. 'Scrub' or

---

17   In what follows about the usage of the word 'bush', I have drawn on historical quotations gathered in Ramson WS (Ed.) (1988) *Australian National Dictionary*. Oxford University Press, Melbourne, pp. 112–119.

'brush' could be dense rainforest, whereas bush was dry and open, and 'forest' could be more open again.

'Forest' is one of the most surprising of colonial words. We think of trees making a forest, but in 19th-century Australia it was grass that made a forest. Although there was some variation in the word's use, 'forest' generally described a woodland area fit to graze. It was a term invested with the pastoral vision. 'Forest' was not impenetrable or difficult to travel through like 'scrub' or 'brush'; it was an open landscape with large trees, little undergrowth and abundant grass. However, surveyors and explorers did distinguish between 'open plains' (treeless grasslands) and 'open forests' (which we now call grassy woodlands). In 1805, 'Forest Land' in New South Wales was 'such as abounds with Grass and is the only Ground which is fit to Graze; according to the local distinction, the grass is the discriminating character and not the Trees, for by making use of the former it is clearly understood as different from a Brush or Scrub'. Many 'forest lands' were not only ideal for grazing, they also produced 'A sufficiency of Grain', and could be ploughed without further clearing. Charles Wilkes, writing for an American audience in 1844, explained that, 'forests' are very different from what we understand by the term, and consist of gum trees (Eucalypti), so widely scattered that a carriage may be driven rapidly through them without meeting any obstruction, while the foliage of these trees is so thin and apparently so dried up as scarcely to cast a shade'. In 1849, Alexander Harris explained that, 'The clear ground changes only into fine open forest, with scarcely a tree to the acre'. When Aboriginal people were dispossessed of their lands and their systematic firestick farming ceased, colonists noticed that many of the open, dry forests they could once ride their horses through became dense and impenetrable.

Steels Creek has harboured all these different kinds of bush. The wind of the flume is written in the trees. As one valley resident put it, 'I have a Red Box tree that is like a banana because it has been shaped by the northerly over 300 years'. The open country of the valley – the 'forest' of the flats – was created and maintained over thousands of years by Aboriginal burning. When the squatters came they found a basin of grassland – a 'park' – that seemed to be a natural range for their introduced animals. Gold miners and selectors cleared the stringybark 'bush' to look for gold and establish small farms. The cessation of Aboriginal burning allowed the dry, open forests to thicken and 'scrub' to grow. Splitters and sawmillers penetrated the ranges in search of messmate, peppermint and grey gum for they needed tall timber to feed the growing metropolis. In the nooks and clefts of the range they found the dense, wet 'brush' of tree fern gullies that increasingly attracted tourists and sojourners. And all this country – this complex, changing mosaic of vegetation and open flats – was and still is 'The Bush' just beyond The City, a pocket of rural life and nature that was never a country town and is still not suburbia.

Wedge-tailed eagles by Margaret McLoughlin.

Landscape across Yarra Valley from Coombe Cottage, Coldstream *by Hans Heysen, 1915 (Courtesy of Nicholas O'Donohue & Co Lawyers). In the summer of 1914-15, Dame Nellie Melba invited Hans Heysen to paint one of her favourite views of the Yarra Valley from her home at Coldstream, near Yarra Glen.*

Steels Creek has retained its rural character. It has resisted being swallowed by the city so near, and the ridgelines of bush still enclose it. It remains a different, distinct world, socially and environmentally. It is, in so many symbolic ways, the quintessential Australian bush. The itinerant pastoral workers of Russel Ward's *The Australian Legend* (1958) were found in this valley: a shearing shed was a social centre for music and yarning, and cattle drives from the north came through the valley. Stock sometimes spent a noisy night corralled in Hunts Lane. Joseph Furphy, bullock-driver, literary champion of the bushman and author of the classic outback novel, *Such is Life* (1903), was born at Yarra Flats (now Yarra Glen) on Ryrie's Station.[18] When an ABC television program, 'For the Juniors', wanted to film a feature on 'country children', they chose Robyn and Derek Schoen and Rick and Sue Arney from Steels Creek as their exemplary rural kids.[19] In 1972 when a schoolteacher and six children were kidnapped from Faraday Primary School in central Victoria, it was the Steels Creek Primary School – a one-teacher school conveniently near the city – that was filmed for news bulletins. In 1981, one of the Creek's homesteads, 'Rose Glen', was chosen as the setting for the film, *I Can Jump Puddles*, an evocation of the bush childhood of beloved writer Alan Marshall. Well into the post-war years this valley so close to Melbourne harboured a simple material existence, the 'vanished Australia' of Geoffrey Blainey's history of daily life, *Bush Kettle and Full Moon* (2003). Steels Creek was late to be embraced by the 20th-century expansion of public services and technology and so it also epitomised the 'Struggle Country' of rural Australia described by historians Graeme Davison and Marc Brodie – the forgotten or marginalised hinterland that for good or ill often feels left behind the nation.[20] Electricity and telephones did not make it to Steels Creek until the late 1950s, by which time television was already established in the cities. Even today there are problems with mobile phone reception in the valley.

---

18   *Yarra Glen & District Historical Society Newsletter* no. 41, November 2011.

19   Arney I (2005) *Steels Creek As I Knew It – 1951-1989*, Yarra Glen & District Historical Society, Publication Series No. 2, p. 25.

20   Davison G and Brodie M (Eds) (2005) *Struggle Country: The Rural Ideal in Twentieth-century Australia*. Monash University ePress, Melbourne.

The society of Steels Creek in the early and mid 20th century is also remarkably reminiscent of the world portrayed by the great poet and storyteller of the Australian bush, Henry Lawson. In this cul-de-sac of the Yarra Valley until barely a lifetime ago were settlers eking out a living in 'the dark, stringy-bark bush'. Lawson was born on the NSW goldfields and 'got bushed' when he went to London, but he did live most of his life in Sydney. He was one of an influential group of writers who, in the late 19th century, found poetic images and lean prose to capture local bush experience for Australian readers and thus fed their strengthening nationalism. Geoffrey Blainey has observed that 'the setting of most of Lawson's stories is in the middle country where the rainfall, while not reliable, was above the Australian average. His country was a mix of hills and flats, mostly fenced in, and hiding deposits of gold here and there.'[21] That sounds just like Steels Creek, often green but subject to drought and constant fire, where boys walking home from school along a dusty road could lose a football down a mining hole. As resident Keith Montell says of early Steels Creek's history, 'the stories are of poverty'. It was a world of alluvial diggings, shallow shafts, gullying creeks, stringybark huts, barn dances, small farms and orchards, pigs and cows, scavenged kerosene-tins and recycled hessian bags. Let us explore the stories of life in this valley, those that have survived in anecdotes, written and spoken reminiscences, snatches of newspaper reports, government records, the fragment of a diary, a letter or two. What was the texture of life in the stringybark bush, who lived here and how are they remembered?[22]

Maria Taylor, who in the early 20th century grew up in Dixons Creek, a small settlement just a few kilometres from Steels Creek, keenly remembered her first holiday. It was a great adventure on foot, when she glimpsed the separate world on the other side of the Pinnacles, the low chain of hills that divides the two communities. From her aunt's place on the Pinnacles, the strange and new Steels Creek valley could be seen.[23] Even in the mid 20th century, these neighbouring settlements were still worlds apart. Vera Adams was a schoolteacher at Dixons Creek who, in 1949, was transferred to Steels Creek. Vera recalled that the Dixons Creek people, who attended a Methodist Church and observed Sundays strictly, warned her that the Steels Creek people were 'a wild lot'. And the Steels Creek folk wanted to know of Vera's experience in distant Dixons Creek: 'How did you get on with those bloody wowsers over there?'[24]

The humble bush settlement of Steels Creek was always dispersed across the flats and foothills and among the trees. As mentioned in Chapter 1, the first selectors (small farmers) arrived in the valley in the late 1860s and goldminers thronged along the creek in 1866–67, bringing the sound of the axe deep into the valley. Alluvial diggings were abandoned because the ground was so wet but these workings were revived and extended in the years following 1893. By 1894, payable gold was being found on more than a dozen claims on Steels Creek and Full and Plenty Creek and about 130 men were living and working there. Some good specimens of gold-studded quartz ('a regular

21   Blainey G (2002) A genius to the fingertips. In: *Henry Lawson*. (Ed. G Blainey) pp. vii–xxxii. Text, Melbourne.
22   In what follows I have drawn on documents gathered by the people of Steels Creek which now form the Steels Creek Community Archive held by the Yarra Glen and District Historical Society, as well as reminiscences of local people in several community workshops we held in November 2010.
23   Taylor FM (1988) *Daughters of Old Steels Creek*. Wilkinson Printers, Albury, pp. 41–42.
24   Adams V (2005) *Steels Creek: A Social History 1946–1995*. Yarra Glen & District Historical Society, Publication Series No. 3, September, p. 1.

jeweller's shop') and even occasionally small nuggets were found among the abandoned claims of the 1860s. 'The scene is romantic and striking as I drive down the gorge late in the afternoon', wrote the Melbourne journalist Julian Thomas (whose pen-name was 'The Vagabond') in May 1894. 'At this point the hills close in until their shadows are blended with those of the towering forest trees. The growth of the timber here is something enormous, and the trees have attained great heights. Across the gorge the mining camp is spread out from north to south. Here and there canvas tents are dotted about. On the slope of the southern hill some slab huts are in course of erection. Everywhere the upper workings of the claims are visible.'[25] One of the chief points in favour of mining in the Steels Creek valley was 'cheapness of timber', which was always essential for windlasses, shafts, accommodation, cooking and warmth.[26] By 1895 about 300 people had employment along the creek.[27] Mines had names such as Pig and Whistle, Porcupine, Napoleon, Ghost Gully, Pinchgut and Black Prince.[28]

Mining at Steels Creek had a reputation of being 'patchy' and the primitive, basic conditions of the first phase of gold-digging remained a permanent state of affairs at the head of the valley. Julian Thomas reported in the *Illustrated Australian News* in 1894 that the 'most primal conditions of early mining life are here observed'. Of the shafts on the banks of the creek he observed that some were 'deserted, some crowned by windlass and coverings of bark'. Even when tents and humpies were being replaced by log huts roofed with bark, the men prepared their evening meal outside: 'some have frying pans, others are boiling corned beef to save further cooking on the morrow, and there is everywhere the inevitable billy of tea'.[29] Thomas was impressed by the 'gallant diggers' and the spectacle of their struggle – with the dirt, flooding water and primitive conditions. 'May the Full and Plenty Creek yield full and plenty gains to them', he declared. 'This digging is altogether so unique – a living object lesson of the earliest life in the goldfields that I suggest it as an enjoyable trip for Melbourne holidaymakers. They can have a day's picnic at Steels Creek as well as a sight of the diggings.' Before the 20th century had even begun and before the colonies had federated into the Commonwealth of Australia, Steels Creek had already become an outdoor museum of Australian history within easy reach of city tourists. One newly launched local mining venture encouraged investment on the basis that the Creek's proximity to Melbourne would enable shareholders to check progress and actually see their money at work.

But it was landowners, orchardists, timber workers and dairy farmers who gradually generated the stability of settlement that created a school in 1886 (for 30 children), a Band of Hope (a temperance organisation) in the same year, a cricket club in 1890, a general store, a church (St Barnabas) and a tiny post office. Although a community had materialised, it was still possible to keep to oneself, for the enshrouding bush created a constellation of private worlds. Only after bushfires could you again see many of your neighbours'

25 *Argus*, 14 May 1894, p. 3.
26 *Argus*, 11 August 1898, p. 7.
27 *Argus*, 8 September 1896, p. 7.
28 For some of the details on mining in the valley we have drawn on *A History of Mining in Steels Creek* compiled by Dr Gordon G Brown (1998) and held in the Steels Creek Community Archive.
29 *The Illustrated Australian News*, 6 January 1894.

houses. Allan Adams remembered how in 'Steels Creek in the old days, nearly everybody down there had a few cows and sold a bit of cream or milk.'[30] On special or momentous occasions a surprising number of people could emerge from the trees or come from further afield, as Steels Creek was reminded on the first market day after Black Saturday. It was the same in June 1928 when 300 people attended a celebration hosted by Councillor Hubbard and his wife in the Yarra Glen Soldiers' Memorial Hall in June 1928. It was William Hubbard's final function as President of the Eltham Shire and doubled as a 21st birthday party for their daughter Doreen (later Doreen Ayres).[31] Of course the evening was mostly devoted to dancing. People again turned out in force to honour the local soldiers after the Second World War. In October 1947, 70 people gathered at the Steels Creek School to honour those who had served abroad. As the *Healesville Guardian* reported, 'Nestling at the foot of Mt. Slide is a tiny place known as Steel's Creek proper. It boasts of nothing more than a church, a school, and an ever so small post office. Yet, on Saturday afternoon last, more than 70 people congregated in the school to see the unveiling of the Honour Board, with 40 names inscribed thereon.'[32]

Until the 1960s when the Melba Highway was opened over the Great Divide, Steels Creek was on the main road north over Mt Slide to Yea and Mansfield. There were just three cars in Steels Creek after the Second World War but log trucks would roll down that dusty road towards Yarra Glen bringing the timber from the ranges, and two buses went each way each day. The baker, butcher and grocer drove their carts and trucks around the homes, taking orders or folding down the tail-piece at the back of the van and cleaving the meat on

William and Elizabeth Hubbard. (Courtesy of Yarra & District Historical Society)

30   Adams, A (1995). Interview by Jo Chirardello, 3 October 1995, typescript in the Steels Creek Community Archive.

31   *Advertiser* (Hurstbridge), 8 June 1928, p. 1.

32   *Healesville Guardian*, 4 October 1947, p. 4.

the spot. On hot days the butcher's wife was his essential companion and her job was to flick the flies away with a gum bough.[33] Charlie Bath, known as 'the Singing Postman', delivered the mail from Yarra Glen each day with his coach and horses and was later helped by his daughters Mary, Phyllis and Ruby. Waiting for the daily mail created the opportunity for small, informal gatherings and for many a lively discussion. Okum, the Indian hawker dressed in a turban, would come every month in a big covered van, selling needles, cotton, cloth and a myriad wonderful things, and camp under the pine trees where he cooked his curried chicken. Gordon Hubbard remembered as a little boy 'looking up into that mysterious interior of his wagon, I was rather frightened at the time but he was a great old guy'.

Steels Creek Community Centre, originally the Primary School, pictured in 2012.

For most of the century between 1886 and 1992, the one-teacher primary school was looked after by just four teachers, such was their commitment to locality. The first teacher, Edward Morris, remained for almost 40 years and established an extensive garden which children remember having to look after. The school always marked Bird Day, Arbor Day and Empire Day, and there was also an annual Beach Day, the much-anticipated trip by train to the sea at Mordialloc or Brighton. Edward Morris was secretary of the Yarra Glen Agricultural and Horticultural Society and a pillar of the community. Doreen Ayres remembered that Mr Morris 'used to wear glasses and if you were playing up in school he could see it.'[34] Years after his death, a diary of his was found under the kitchen linoleum of his house by a new owner. A week of entries revealed that, on one occasion, Mr Morris stabbed his foot with a garden fork, suffered days of pain, tried home remedies and then lived in hope that a doctor would be at Kinglake the following Saturday. The week's final entry read: 'Walked to Kinglake today [about 9 km up a steep mountain road], doctor not there, waited three hours, walked home, arriving after dark, foot still very painful.' The diary has since gone missing again.[35]

Next door to the school was a little post office that was open every day and on Saturday mornings, and it was always kept active round the clock during any bushfire. It was the crucial communication centre. Before electricity and telephone lines made their way up the valley – and even by 1960 they did not go all the way – people could make calls from the post office. Anyway, as Barbara Hunt Harris put it, 'the bush telegraph was faster than telephones!'

33   Sadlier F *My Reminiscences of Yarra Glen since 1915*. Compiled and edited by Leigh Ahern. Yarra Glen & District Historical Society, Publication Series no. 4, August 2006, p. 14.

34   Ayres D (1995), Conversation with Helen and Tim Todhunter, 9 September 1995, typescript in the Steels Creek Community Archive.

35   The four teachers whose appointments to the school made a total of almost 80 years were: Edward Morris (1886-1921), Frank Livingstone (1946-55), Vera Adams (1955-73) and Irene Meredith (1973-86). Adams V (1986) *Steels Creek Primary School No. 2725, 1886–1986*. School Centenary Committee, Steels Creek.

Rose Glen barn in 2011.

Nearly opposite the school was the Rose Glen barn, owned for a time by the Siggins family, where flower shows, dances and social evenings were held. The barn was earlier a shearing shed and then was used to store hay. 'Once the hay was out … in with the dance', remembered Doreen Ayres. 'We used to do the floors up with sawdust with kerosene in it.'[36] On moonlit nights, the Adams brothers would play the piano accordion, Harold ('Snowy') Hunt sang 'Ah! Sweet mystery of life' and the younger children would sleep the night away on the hay. Doreen retained a vivid image of Frank Livingstone, the Steels Creek schoolteacher from 1946 to 1955, dancing nimbly on top of a 44-gallon drum, all 18 stone of him.

Northwards and past a fork and bend of the road was a general store on the corner of Hunts Lane. It was stocked from local suppliers as well as a weekly trip to the Victoria Market in Melbourne and children knew it had a cellar for soft drinks. In the interwar years it was owned by Robert and Violet Hunt. 'Everything happened here', remembered Barbara Hunt Harris: it is where locals came to spin a yarn, complain about Mr Lyons, Mr Chifley or Mr Menzies, and where the sweep for the Melbourne Cup was drawn. Guy Fawkes Night and Bonfire Night were held nearby. In summer, people got their water from the creek (children remembered it later as clear and delicious) and everyone learned to swim there in the pool just below the bridge. When the house water tanks were low, Violet Hunt and Edna Collinson did their washing on the banks by lighting a fire under an old kerosene tin. Violet also fished for blackfish there.

The Steels Creek cricket and tennis clubs were vital centres of community activity and patriotism, and the tennis club remains important today. In the 1890s and the first two-thirds of the 20th century, Steels Creek (thanks to the likes of the Hubbard and Morris boys, the three Adams brothers and Tom Thompson) punched well above its weight in the local cricket competition, regularly vanquishing Kinglake, Toolangi, Coldstream, Yumbunga, Yarra Glen and Dixons Creek and winning premierships. The opposing teams were 'pretty good cricketers', recalled Allan Adams: 'they would bring a nine gallon [keg] with them, you couldn't see the ball in the finish.'[37] Right from the beginning cricket had strong local support. In January 1890, the day before the first match of the Steels Creek Cricket Club (against Yarra Glen), the Creek's first farmer George Fletcher offered a sucking pig to be raffled to the benefit of

36   Ayres D, Conversation with Helen and Tim Todhunter.
37   Adams, A, Interview by Jo Chirardello.

the Cricket Club, Mr Flanagan gave one guinea for the best batsman and Mr Hubbard half a guinea for the best bowler.[38] 'The Glenites', in spite of being an old established club, won by only three runs. The first pitch was laid on the flats below Rose Glen with sand from the gold mines. Later, a concrete pitch was installed and it is still down there on the flats, invisible but not forgotten.

Cricket is responsible for the most mentions of Steels Creek in the published historical record; it hits any other subject for six. On weekends, sawmillers, engine-drivers and farmers became famous for their deadly batting, wily hat-tricks and balletic fielding. Vera Adams remembers how wives, sisters and girlfriends knew that cricket always came first: 'More than one burgeoning romance ended because "she couldn't stand cricket, wouldn't even try to get used to it."'[39] So women generally pitched in, baked legendary sponge cakes, and even for a time had a ladies' team, although Vera did remember that, while serving dutifully on the sidelines, she often wished a stonewalling batsman would go out or the rain would start again. Mrs Morris prepared tea for each home match in a four-gallon tin (or billy) hung on a tripod over an open fire. There were regular matches in the valley between married and single men. Ern Cary, once a fine footballer, was later the local cricket umpire and took care to bring the sacred traditions of the game to the little field among the gums. Insisting on strict deportment and behaviour, he was scandalised in 1946 when young Clyde Plant, a newcomer and a dairy farmer from Pinnacle Lane, stepped onto the field in neat white shorts instead of the requisite longs. The game with Toolangi almost didn't proceed. It was the first match after the war and excitement was running high; the

The creek today near Hunts Lane.

38 *Evelyn Observer*, 10 January 1890, p. 3.

39 Adams V, *Steels Creek*: A Social History, p. 6.

pre-war premiership shields had been burnt in the school fire of 1943, new equipment had been purchased, livestock had been removed from the oval in preparation for the great day, and the men from Toolangi were getting restless. Ern Cary gave in.[40] As well as serving as cricket umpire, Ern would often dress as Santa for the schoolkids, clambering up the hill into the bush behind the school to don his gear. (One year Ted Lancaster, a pensioner living in a hut by the creek, was Santa, but he had to wear gloves because the children would have spotted that he lacked a telltale couple of fingers.)[41]

Each year, the Steels Creek community held a Sports Day on the cricket ground, and ice cream was brought in especially for the event. All sorts of competitions were featured: woodchopping, foot and barrow races, stepping the chain, quoits, walking with a blindfold, bowling at a single stump, tossing a sheaf of hay over a bar and hammering a nail into hard wood. One year, Ivy Arney remembers having just a shilling to spend and, having been a builder's labourer on the family home, she ran the nail through her hair first and hammered it home, winning two shillings and sixpence to spend at other events. Ted Lancaster won a hot-water bottle, the first he'd ever owned.[42]

Henry Lawson's evocation of the bush was, above all, a social one. In portraying the land's harshness, he exalted the humans who forbore it. He had an eye for the rituals and customs of raw settlement and for the rugged, eccentric individuals who struggled to make a living from marginal land and an uncertain climate. The bush community gave such people space, privacy, affectionate respect and, if they were sick or old, occasional support. Steels Creek had its share of these characters, remembered for their idiosyncrasies and their acts of kindness. 'Old Tom Clements' was said to be related to Mark Twain (Samuel Clements) and he had a dugout in the bank of Full and Plenty Creek before 1939, and a hut too. He would come to the shop and talk and spit, and as soon as he left they washed the road with buckets of water. He owned a bike made of wood (pictured on p. 64). Jack Calwell delivered the bread twice a week in the war years and capped any transaction with a memorable, seamless phrase: 'Yesmywordtooright!' 'Old Man Riddell' (Robert), still mining in the post-war period, was considered 'a red ragger', a communist. His politics were manifest in those regular community conversations outside the little post office. He had a wife and two children and although they lived in primitive conditions, you would never have known it. She dressed herself and the children 'like out of a band box' and was a wonderful cook.

William and Ellen Hunt married in 1869 and were among the earliest white settlers at Steels Creek, and over the years the valley was populated with the exploits and nicknames of their children and nephews and nieces. The two Robert Hunts were differentiated as Black Bob (or Long Bob) and Red Bob, and there was also Button Hunt, Snowy Hunt and Auntie Fan. There was Lincoln Hunt (named after Abraham), Bernard Hunt (named after Shaw) and Vincent Hunt (named after Van Gogh). There were also the descendants of David Rolfe who came to farm in Steels Creek in 1868, and the family of Edward Collinson and Margaret Hunt who married in 1896, ran cows, cut wood and raised three boys and four girls. One of their sons, Reg Collinson, was a top notch blacksmith, and it was said he could make a horseshoe in five minutes. In the

40   Adams V, *Steels Creek: A Social History*, pp. 6–7.

41   Arney I, *Steels Creek As I Knew It*, p. 14.

42   Arney I (2005) *Steels Creek as I knew it, 1951–1989*. Yarra Glen & District Historical Society, Yarra Glen.

early days, many of the children born in the valley and the forest beyond were delivered by Ellen Hunt. Meryl Collinson remembers that it was not unknown for Ellen to travel by jinker and lantern light as far as Queenstown (near St Andrews) to help at a birth. Grannie Hunt (known by everyone as Auntie Nellie) lived on her own after her husband died; she skinny-dipped in the creek, killed snakes, and kept a shotgun in the hut, with which she was known to scare away small, annoying boys (often named Adams). Button Hunt's wife, Auntie Fan, had a pipe organ in her house and would get local lads to pump it while she played. Her house was full of music and she sang with a beautiful contralto voice. Long Bob, who kept the store, built part of the Mt Slide Road up to the Kinglake ridge – 'a mile of the Slide' – in the early 1920s. Snowy Hunt – who sang those moonlit nights away in the Rose Glen barn – was one of three searchers who, on 4 January 1955, located a plane that crashed in tall gum trees when coming in low over Mt Slide above Steels Creek. In places it took up to two and a half hours for the searchers to travel half a mile in that forest. The pilot and two passengers died and the plane's wreckage was scattered down the steep mountainside. Nothing of the crash could be seen from the air so Snowy and his mates, having found the wreckage, lit a fire to signal its whereabouts, a tricky strategy in January. More than 40 rescuers worked to bring out the bodies.[43]

The state of the narrow, steep road up the ridge to Kinglake was a constant source of local anxiety, politics and complaint. Even in the early 1920s, settlers trying to get their produce to market could spend much of their time on the road, ploughing through the mud, avoiding ruts a metre deep that extended for hundreds of metres.[44] In 1910, the horses of the mail coach going up the Old Kinglake Road became entangled with a team of bullocks attached to a wagon coming down and the coach was overturned, throwing and badly injuring the driver, and narrowly avoiding the plunge into the valley below.[45] In 1951, Vera Adams and her spellbound children rounded a sharp bend on the Mt Slide Road and encountered the caravans of a circus struggling up the steep incline. The vehicles had encountered difficulties and the circus elephant was being put to good use.[46]

Alf Swift, also known as Arty Sparkles or Swifty – or 'Jonathan' to the literary schoolteacher, Mr Morris – lived alone on Mt Slide. When his home was burnt down, he looked after someone else's empty house. He was a fruit grower and ran cattle in the bush; they would come when he called. He came down to the Creek every week on his pony to get food from the grocer's cart in Hunts Lane and he also called at Button Hunt's place for eggs, letting the family know he was there by banging a stick on the water tank. The miners in the valley looked forward to his visit so that they could provoke a brawl, but Swifty fought like a threshing machine and always cleaned them up. Alf was renowned for appearing in Steels Creek late on polling day, insisting he could vote there rather than Kinglake where he was registered. 'I can vote anywhere in Australia and you can't stop me.'[47]

43   *Argus*, 5 January 1955.

44   *Advertiser* (Hurstbridge), 27 October 1922, p. 2.

45   *Argus*, 18 March 1910, p. 8.

46   Adams V, *Steels Creek: A Social History*, p. 15.

47   As told to Meryl Collinson by Lincoln William Hunt, 24 January 2001.

Vera Adams offered the following mid-century memory of 'possibly the most eccentric of several unforgettable Steels Creek characters'. George and Frank Murray were two brothers who did not mix with their neighbours but were remembered for their distinctive shearing season. 'The Murrays', wrote Vera, 'had a few sheep, grey and tattered, not unlike their owners … There was no shearing shed or sheep yards. I cannot remember any dog being involved. The brothers removed a door from within the house and put it on the ground in the backyard. They then set about capturing a sheep, ambling around the paddock, with ragged coats billowing, weird cries uttered from a distance suggesting some sort of medieval chant or spell, but people who got close enough said there was no wizardry involved. The elder man kept up a continuous stream of abuse in very colourful language, at his brother, the sheep, or both. The sheep were in no better condition than the men, inevitably a poor panting creature would collapse to be seized and dragged to the "board". Shearing with old blade shears wielded by two operators still took considerable time … The chase and the flow of invective continued until twilight made further activity impossible, and it all began again in the early morning.'[48]

These are all handed-down, much-loved stories of the valley. They are, of course, very selective and dwell on eccentricities and humour. Therefore they offer us a colourful caricature of local life, capturing the basic conditions of rural living which long persisted, and depicting hardship, bloodymindedness and a capacity for fun. They present a portrait of a community caught in an apparently timeless moment that, in some stories, could be anywhere between 1890 and 1960. But they preserve glimpses of real people, named and beloved, and they vividly evoke a genuine historical era when community institutions had materialised out of the ebb and flow of squatting and gold-digging but before electricity, the motor car, the telephone and the highway began to change the material, economic and demographic character of the place.

But over the years and still today, Steels Creek has remained a dispersed settlement among the trees, a bush community. There are more houses in the valley now but less public infrastructure than a century ago. People still emerge from the trees to play, party and help one another, while others are rarely seen except in crisis. And residents of the valley today are perhaps more aware than ever of the beauty of the place, and of the value of nature in their lives.

Gumsuckers

If people from New South Wales were popularly known as 'Cornstalks', South Australians as 'Croweaters', Queenslanders as 'Bananalanders' or 'Bananabenders', and Western Australians as 'Sandgropers', then the distinguishing environmental fate of Victorians was that they were 'Gumsuckers'. Whether sucking sweet gum from the trunks of wattles, or simply growing up among the gum trees, colonial Victorians were identified as forest dwellers.

The first Europeans to venture deep into the tall forests of the Yarra Valley regarded the trees with awe. They were different from the intensively used woodlands on Victoria's central goldfields and western plains. The special character of these steeper, wetter, denser, taller mountain forests was

48   Adams V, *Steels Creek: A Social History*, p. 2.

expressed in the forms of the soaring mountain ash, the delicate tree fern, the rainforest beech, and the theatrical and cheeky lyrebird. These distinctive features captured the popular imagination and have persisted as symbols of the Yarra Ranges. Some colonists regarded the lushness and magic of the mountain forests as almost un-Australian; here the oft-derided eucalypt was actually impressive, and the massive ferns seemed tropical and mystical.

In 1858, Alfred Howitt stood in wonder under tree ferns in the Dandenongs and reflected that it was 'one of those tropical looking spots one would rather expect to find in the south seas than in Australia … We ought to have been a thousand miles away from Melbourne instead of 20, so wild and solitary was the scene.'[49] When, from 1862, the Yarra Track was opened up to the mountain goldfields of the east (Jamieson, Woods Point, Matlock and Walhalla), miners, packers and storekeepers surged up the Yarra Valley, camped along its banks, watered their horses at the river and marvelled over the 'perfect jungle' that clothed the higher ridges. One traveller compared it with the delightful scenery of Ceylon. He enjoyed 'the sweet smelling freshness of the ferns', some of which towered over 10 metres above him. Both of Victoria's faunal emblems, the helmeted honeyeater (*Lichenostomus melanops cassidix*) and Leadbeater's possum (*Gymnobelideus leadbeateri*), are only found in or near the Yarra Ranges – and both are endangered. The superb lyrebird (*Menura novaehollandiae*) has a wide distribution throughout south-eastern Australia, but Melbourne's Sherbrooke Forest – on the southern face of the Dandenongs – became its most famous home. International visitors to the city were taken into the hills to glimpse the lyrebird's display and hear its mimicry, and to gaze up the white boles of the tallest mountain ash.

The first 'camping-out' excursion of the Field Naturalists' Club of Victoria was held at Olinda Creek in the Dandenongs in November 1884, four years after the club's foundation. 'All departments of natural history were represented' at the gathering and the group included A.J. Campbell and the photographer Nicholas Caire. The first day 'Being Sunday the guns were left behind till the morrow'. But by the following morning, the party was so bristling with arms that new arrivals 'were at first afraid they had been conducted into the midst of a band of Italian banditti, so varied and formidable looking were the clothes and weapons of the party'.[50] The ornithologists were particularly triumphant 'in taking for the first time the nest and eggs of the rare and certainly the most beautiful of all the Australian honey-eaters', the helmeted honeyeater.[51]

By the early 20th century, the Yarra Ranges were the stage for enacting new sensibilities towards nature. Twenty years after the Field Naturalists' Club's first excursion of armed 'banditti' to Olinda Creek, three young nature-lovers – Charles Barrett, Claude Kinane and Brooke Nicholls – established camp at a bush hut in the same valley. Inspired by Henry Thoreau, they named their hut 'Walden'. But, as Barrett put it, 'Unlike our Master, we paid taxes, having no Emerson to pay them for us; and also, we welcomed visitors, which Thoreau seldom did.'[52] Their plan was to spend all their weekends and holidays there and to monitor carefully, in words and photos, the natural history of their neighbourhood.

49   AW Howitt to Anna Mary Howitt, 15 January 1858, quoted in Bonyhady T (2000) *The Colonial Earth*. Melbourne University Press, Melbourne, p. 107.

50   The 'camp out' at Olinda Creek. *Victorian Naturalist* **1** (1884–85), 110–112.

51   Land Conservation Council (1994) *Melbourne Area District 2 Review: Final Recommendations*. LCC, Melbourne, p. 96.

52   Barrett C (1939) *Koonwarra: A Naturalist's Adventures in Australia*. Oxford University Press, London, p. 35.

Barrett wrote in 1905 that '[w]e desired to experience that return to Nature of which so much has been written in recent years; to leave the din and dust of the great city, and dwell awhile in the forest among birds and flowers and trees.'[53] Their hut, set in the midst of an old orchard near Olinda Creek and a pleasant walk from the Lilydale railway station, was a base for bird-watching, plant identification, photography, a daily notation of observations, and plenty of yarning and letter writing. Once ensconced in their chosen valley in the Dandenongs, the three nature-lovers were quick to compare it with the 'hill, dale, woodland and water' of Gilbert White's famous English parish of Selborne. They called themselves 'The Woodlanders', thereby invoking another recorder of rural ways, Thomas Hardy, whose novel of that name was published in 1887.

The opening of the railway to Yarra Glen in 1888 brought an increasing number of tourists to the Steels Creek valley in search of accessible but exotic bushland. 'The Vagabond' enthused in 1893 that the mountains of the Healesville district 'cast a moral spell' on all visitors, drawing them back.[54] Enterprising locals established guesthouses in Greenwood Lane and Hunts Lane and opened walking tracks. Steels Creek's location under the Kinglake escarpment meant that the mystical fern forests were part of its identity. In September 1903, when Mr Ern Cary married Miss Janet Hubbard in the Church of England at Steels Creek, bride and bridesmaids carried bouquets of ferns and white flowers. In 1913, new fern bowers were discovered along Full and Plenty Creek and there was cooperation between the local timber industry

and the Yarra Glen Progress Association in celebrating and advertising the beauty of the bush. Bushmen seeking more timber on the slopes of Mt Slide had found 'fern gullies of exquisite beauty' and soon people were led along the old timber tram tracks and up the ridge beside the mountain streams to a place of 'dense growth overhead, through which sunlight rarely entered'. The brown fern trunks were from 6 to 9 metres high and created 'a lofty roof of broad-branching tree fronds'.[55] Three weeks later, on 12 February, the Progress Association hosted a picnic there and 100 people made the journey to admire what many said was the most beautiful fern gully they had ever seen. 'Cameras were, as usual, much in evidence.' The bower was declared open and named Gordon Glade after the manager of the nearby Ewanburn sawmill.[56]

Ewanburn sawmill. (Courtesy of Yarra Glen & District Historical Society)

53   'The woodlanders' [Charles Barrett], 'Our bush hut on Olinda', Parts 1–5, *The New Idea: A Woman's Home Journal for Australasia*, October, November, December, 1905, January, February 1906. The quote is from the issue of 6 October 1905, p. 354. See also Barrett CL and Nicholls EB (March 1905) Bird notes from Olinda Vale. *Victorian Naturalist* **21**(11), 162–166; Barrett CL (August 1906) Bird life on Olinda Creek. *Victorian Naturalist* **23**(4), 84–89; and Nicholls EB (February 1907) Excursion to Olinda Vale. *Victorian Naturalist* **23**(10), 172–173.

54   *Healesville Guardian*, 29 December 1893, p. 4.

55   *Healesville and Yarra Glen Guardian*, 17 January 1913, p. 3.

56   *Healesville and Yarra Glen Guardian*, 21 February 1913, p. 2.

While the fern bower was being celebrated, splitters were still taking the tallest trees in the forests on the ridge and 'to naturalists it was sad to see the destruction of forest giants going on in every direction'.[57] But the development of tourism and walking tracks often proceeded hand in hand with other uses of the bush. Sawmillers sometimes offered hikers a cup of tea, or the scouts some training in bush skills. When a party of naturalists sheltered from a hailstorm in a sawmill near Warburton, the mill workers showed off their handiwork of whittling walking sticks from blackwood.[58] Miners' and splitters' tracks provided routes for walkers, and some of the timber tramways doubled as tourist trips or attractive picnic strolls almost from their inception. Timber tramways were the linear habitats along which naturalists collected. Tourists could themselves threaten the beauty of the bush. As the *Lilydale Express* noted in 1926, 'Given unfettered liberty in the matter of robbing nature of her treasures in plant life, and a horde of tourists will strip the finest gullies and hills of all their charm in a very little time'.[59]

From the 1920s, the promotion and declaration of Kinglake National Park strengthened the protection of fern gullies, tall trees and waterfalls and increased the scenic fame of the region. In 1928, the year the park was officially gazetted, keen bushwalker and writer, R.H. Croll, celebrated 'a delightful woodland way through a forest of messmate which has lately known a bush fire'. 'That should have ruined its beauty', he continued, 'but has only enhanced it. The trunks are a rich black and the tops have gained new tones, while the road is spread with leaves more thickly than any autumn glade in Vallombrosa [Tuscany]'.[60] Thus the region offered city sojourners not only scenic splendour but also an education in fire. A 1913 tourist guide to the Narbethong and Marysville districts featured a cover photo of 'A Bush Fire on Mt Dom Dom'.[61] Although a distant bushfire might be considered a spectacle, rampant firestorms were definitely bad for business. The 1926 fire induced a tremendous slump in the guesthouse business of the Yarra Valley: 'Every day has brought shoals of cancellations from intending visitors', reported the *Lilydale Express* in early March.[62] Visitors to the Healesville district were 'more than a little disturbed by the "pillars of fire by night and clouds of smoke by day"'.

In the early and mid 20th century, there was some modest money to be made in the Steels Creek valley by the selling of firewood for Melbourne – and also of gum tips. Evelyn Smith recalled how people would clip off the new gum tips, make them into big bundles, load them in the truck and sell them at the flower market in the city. 'Most houses', she remembered, 'sported floral arrangements of gum tips in a large vase – no flowers, just the long, bunched tips. The new tips glowed red and the leaves gave off a clean fresh scent – very trendy'.[63]

57   Barnard FGA (February 1910) Excursion to Toolangi. *Victorian Naturalist* **26**(10), 144–150.
58   Barnard FGA (December 1905) Excursion to Warburton. *Victorian Naturalist* **22**(8), 128–132.
59   *Lilydale Express*, 5 March 1926, p. 2.
60   Quoted in Lennon J (1992) Kinglake National Park. In: *Secrets of the Forest: Discovering History in Melbourne's Ash Range*. (Ed. T Griffiths) p. 196. Allen & Unwin, Sydney.
61   *Tourists Map of Narbethong and Marysville Districts*. Victoria, Department of Lands and Survey, Melbourne, 1913.
62   *Lilydale Express*, 5 March 1926, p. 2.
63   Howden M (1999) *Community Life in Yarra Glen: Evelyn Smith's Story*. Mary Howden, Melbourne.

Towards the end of the 20th century, as a new wave of settlers moved into the valley, the bush continued to offer Steels Creek residents livelihood, identity, companionship, shelter, social sanctuary and natural wonders. Dorothy Barber and her family were attracted to Steels Creek because 'we could live as an extended family, grow our own fruit and vegies, have access to schools. The nature was a bonus.' Her grandchildren had a worm farm and there was also an echidna that ranged between Dorothy's house and that of her daughter, Nicole. 'I would be woken by the echidna burrowing for ants', recalled Dorothy. 'And you find yourself looking forward to the orchids.'[64] Jenny Barnett was an orchid expert and led the local 'Clamberers' group on orchid walks.

David Allan and his wife Robyn moved to Steels Creek from the suburbs at the very end of the 20th century and were attracted by the nature of the bush in the valley: 'open, not too dense, no middle-storey, you could walk through it – we didn't want mountain ash forest which was too dark and dangerous. And we learned early that this place got done over in the 60s [the 1962 fire].' They were soon welcomed to their new home by the kookaburras. 'Each spring and summer you'd hear a great cacophony in the valley and the parent birds would bring the young ones up to the house … The silence was something we came to value. You could hear the kookaburra breathing after it had flown up from the valley, and the claws of the treecreeper climbing up a trunk, the call of the bronzewing pigeons.'

The eerie silence that followed Black Saturday was very different. No leaves to stir in the breeze, no birds singing, no scratching animals. But life was determined. Jane Calder remembered: 'The second morning after the fire, a whipbird called. We woke Monday, Tuesday, Wednesday to the sound of a whipbird calling.' And Dorothy rejoiced when the bellbirds were back. 'We didn't notice them so much before the fires but now they are singing constantly.'

Hannah Sky lives near the National Park and, before Black Saturday, had an old miner's cottage, fruit trees and a community of animals. 'I never ever felt lonely living in that house because it was full of creatures. So many brushytails! When they were bored, they'd gnaw on the rafters and the whole house would vibrate! They and their descendants lived in the house for years. "Pisserpossum" was one we'd raised from a baby and he lived in a box in a tree. There was a family of ringtails. They were always there. They were very well behaved, the sweetest little creatures. The first coincidence of a bit of warmth in the spring and a full moon, and they'd spend the whole night galloping up and down the roof. Apart from that outburst of exuberance, they were so well behaved. One of the things that I find hardest to bear is that those little creatures are gone [after the fire]. We battled constantly with bush rats, and every summer one would die in the walls and you either had to live through it or pull out the walls. Once, something fell out of the ceiling into my hair, and it was maggots spilling from a dead bush rat! I abandoned the house. That's one thing about the fires … I thought: "Got the bloody bush rats!"'

---

64   Quotes from Steels Creek residents in this and following paragraphs are drawn from a Community Workshop held for this project in the Steels Creek Community Centre in November 2010.

The creek behind Hannah's house was a source of constant joy to her and her son, Wirrun. 'If it had been raining, you could hear the creeks running, it was a beautiful thing to hear. You'll see a creek and it's a dry gully and you know that water will flow again – it's symbolic of renewal. For many years it flowed every year and we'd spend all summer there in pools, making little dams. We could catch galaxiid fish and keep them in a bucket for a day, and catch tiger leeches. There was "the Dragon Pool" with three logs shaped like dragons, and "the Long Pool" where there was a big rock called a syncline, the "Megiemoo Pool" named after a niece, all named places we could walk to or swim in. The creek was the constant sound of living in that house. At the end of summer it might go dry for a few weeks, and when it would go dry, you'd *hear* the silence! And after rain it was like a storm-drain, a surf beach, BOOM! You could hear the rocks moving underwater. When Wirrun was a teenager, we wondered if we should move away, but then we thought: "But what about the creek? You just couldn't leave the creek." When I first moved there in 1983, we drank from the creek and washed in it too – it was very cold and very beautiful. Three weeks after the bushfire there was the rain and it's hardly stopped flowing.'

Locals monitored local nature lovingly and, where necessary, assertively (regular invocations to destroy European wasps appeared in *The Jolly Thing*). There was pride in the identification of a bent-wing bat colony in one of the mining shafts on Mt Slide. Late in 1998, a fledgling powerful owl was tagged in Steels Creek and almost three years later, it was found feeding on a rat in the Royal Botanical Gardens in Melbourne – 'possibly the only record of the movement of a tagged powerful owl' and therefore worthy of note in the local newsletter. Malcolm Calder observed that, 'The bush became part of your garden.' And Jane Calder reflected that, 'This place drew people who really responded to the environment, who didn't just wander through it but wanted to make it part of themselves and their lives.'.

* * *

One Sunday afternoon in the autumn of 1946, Vera Adams walked over Pinnacle Lane from Dixons Creek and first gazed down upon Steels Creek. She had grown up near Horsham on the flat, dry plains of the Wimmera and taught in the Mallee during years of drought. She was 'overawed' by Dixons Creek valley until the day she ventured over the Pinnacles and saw Steels Creek. She looked with wonder on 'intensely green fields, the splash of autumn colour in a small grove of persimmon trees on the facing slope, the soft olive green of the nearer tree-covered hills, and the deep dark blue of the distant mountains. I had never seen anything like it.' She was entranced by the 'soft gentle landscape'.[65]

The lovely mixture of paddock and forest, mountain and flats, green and olive has constantly drawn people to visit and inhabit Steels Creek. It is real Australian bush, so accessible, yet also benign in appearance. It was a place where European immigrants could more easily and quickly feel at home. The Steels Creek landscape, apparently soft and gentle, can be disarmingly seductive. All the more shocking, then, was the rogue, violent force that erupted from the forest. Those overseas immigrants who first settled in the

---

65   Adams V, *Steels Creek: A Social History*, p. 1.

valley in the 19th century brought a familiarity with demanding weather and rural hardship but they had never before experienced the might and terror of a wind-driven bushfire. Fire reminded them that, however green was their valley, they lived in the bush, and they were Australians.

'Tangled leaves' by Malcolm Calder, painted three weeks after the fire.

A permanent fresh water spring flows into a small dam just north of Uplands Road on Steels Creek Road, not far from the Yarra Glen intersection. The horse trough, installed in 1913 to catch water from the spring, was considered the border of the Steels Creek locality until it was removed in the late 20th century. It was an irresistible temptation for the 14-year-old Myrna Kennedy in 1934, as she dabbled her bare feet in the water. According to Allan Adams, the local lads also found it a handy cooling off spot on the way home from the pub.

Life in the valley

Myrna Kennedy, taken by Dorothy Walker, 1934.
(Courtesy of Yarra Glen & District Historical Society)

Edward C. Morris was a man of many roles – teacher, gardener, photographer, postmaster and temperance enthusiast amongst them. He arrived in Steels Creek in 1886, a fresh 28-year-old, as inaugural headmaster at the newly instituted single-room country school. The position suited him perfectly – as much for the garden plot that came with the teacher's quarters as for the job itself. Mr Morris had clearly been dying to get his hands dirty. If reading, writing and arithmetic were the order of the day indoors, it was digging, weeding and watering that dominated outside. The temperate climate, ample rainfall and sunny aspect fitted his gardening ambitions very nicely. And having a team of small, although not always willing, volunteers at his disposal – many of them his own offspring – allowed him to work on an impressive scale. Apple and pear orchards flanked the small schoolhouse and garden beds spilled from his family residence across the fence to fill the entire acre block. Persimmons, plums, peaches and vegetables both fed and infuriated generations of school children. As one ex-pupil put it, 'We inherited that flaming garden when we went to school!'

Edward Morris (1858–1933).
First schoolmaster at Steels Creek (1886–1922).
Founder and Secretary of Yarra Glen Agricultural and Horticultural Society and Show (1901–1920).
He was also a keen photographer, rumoured to use one of the mines at the back of the school as a darkroom. (Courtesy of Yarra Glen & District Historical Society)

Mrs Morris and children in garden surrounding the teacher's house.
(From the collection of Margaret Crozier)

Each year there was an annual flower show with prizes for categories such as best posy, best saucer, best arrangement. There were no restrictions on collecting flowers from the bush in those days – pincushions, everlastings, heath, bluebells, orchids, salt and pepper. The judging was done in Rose Glen barn with all the flowers arranged at one end of the hall. After the judging the band would start up and the dance would begin. Harold Hunt, who had a beautiful voice, would sing 'Ah, sweet mystery of life', and Dick Adams would play the accordion.

Hedley Ellis Snr with a work truck and a bunch of gum tips which he sold to the market in Melbourne. These were very much in vogue and people would go home from their weekend trip with a bunch.

Standing in Auntie Nellie's front yard with bunches of wild flowers, 1933.
From left to right Daisy, Beryl Plumb (née Hunt), Hilma Smedley (née Hunt), Myrtle House, in front
Meryl Collinson (née Plumb). (From the collection of Meryl Collinson)

(From the collection of Barbara Hunt Harris)

The five Hunt brothers standing on the bridge crossing Steels Creek, circa late 1800s.

Long Bob was a renowned trickster and loved to laugh; it is not clear if he was demonstrating the real depth of the creek or was on his knees.

(From the collection of Meryl Collinson)

Robert Hunt (Long Bob) checking the depth of the water in Steels Creek, circa 1930s.
(From the collection of Barbara Hunt Harris)

On a hot day the family would sit under the willow tree and the kids would take a dip.

Outside 'Fairview', the Collinsons' house (first on the right in Old Kinglake Road), circa 1911.

Meryl Plum, Hedley and Barbara Harris paddle in the creek while the adults watch.
On Hunt's property, at the corner of Hunt's Lane and Steels Creek Road, circa early 1930s.
(From the collection of Barbara Hunt Harris)

From left to right: Albert Hunt, Harold Burgess, Ellen Hunt (née O'Connors), Eliza Beams Burgess with baby, William Hunt, Robert Alfred Hunt (Red Bob) on horse and Shirley Hunt sitting.
(From the collection of Meryl Collinson)

Healesville Guardian 17 January 1913

FERN BOWERS DISCOVERED – YARRA GLEN DISTRICT.
Members of the Yarra Glen Progress League Committee … have been led through bush maze to a fern-bower where, till very recently, no human foot has trod.

The League committee set out on Sunday morning to 'explore' and in the journey some fern gullies of exquisite beauty were met. After driving to the site of Gordon's old sawmill … a course was taken up the gully along the old timber tram tracks, to the Full and Plenty Creek … [T]he party was rewarded by the sight of a fern bower of exceeding beauty.

Several interesting bowers, large and small, were passed on the upward journey; there was a dense growth overhead, through which sunlight rarely entered; logs and rocks were damp and moss-covered and it was difficult to maintain a footing …

Two mountain streams of clear, icy-cold water murmured their way towards the distant Yarra beneath a lofty roof of broad-branching fern fronds. The brown fern trunks were from 20 to 30 feet high, relieved by the varying shades of green of moss inches deep, native creepers, stag ferns, and coils of supple jack. Festoons of native creepers clung to the trunks, and linked the group while underfoot there were several varieties of small fern well known to bushmen.

Hazel, blackwood, and Christmas bush were there, lending their beauty to the spot. There were also some smaller gullies of interest. Before making the return journey the party ascended Mount Slide from which an extensive panoramic view of the surrounding country was obtained.

It is intended to cut tracks to facilitate access to the gullies and a picnic will be held to celebrate their opening at an early date.

Burt Miller, Ted Smith, Vic Flintoff and Sam Smith at 'Modesty Farm' on Pinnacle Lane (nowadays known as Blackwood Hill), circa 1949.

Sam Smith sawing firewood, late 1940s.

Left: Road making gang at the quarry on Mount Slide Road. Tom Irvine is holding the horse. Early 1920s.

Right: Jack Barton, a visitor from the city, making use of the ensuite washing facilities.

(Courtesy of Yarra Glen & District Historical Society)

(From the collection of Barbara Hunt Harris)

Friends from Melbourne on a weekend hunting expedition.

Orchards were grown on many properties along the Steels Creek Road, but none better than those planted by the Hubbard family. The apples and pears grown on their 30-acre Pinnacle Lane farm were exported to Europe and won many prizes at international competitions. Gordon Hubbard remembered 'The first truck we bought was to market the fruit and it was my job to pay for it by cartage during the week.'

(From the collection of Barbara Hunt Harris)

Apple packers on Morris's orchard circa early 1900s. Vera Morris is on the right.
(From the collection of Margaret Crozier)

Long Bob at Tom Clements' camp, riding Tom's home-made wooden bike. The camp was below Mt Slide Road on Full and Plenty Creek.

Gwenneth 'Queenie' Pitchford was the teacher at Steels Creek from 1943 to 1946. The school building burnt down during her time, destroying all the records of past pupils.

(From the collection of Meryl Collinson)

'Queenie' on her motorbike.
(From the collection of Barbara Hunt Harris)

Hedley Ellis, 1929.

Ted, Laurie and Robin with their father Sam Smith, late 1940s.

(From the collection of Barbara Hunt Harris)

(From the collection of Barbara Hunt Harris)

Inside William David (Button) Hunt's house circa 1939.

St Barnabas church, circa 1940s. The church was never consecrated. Eventually it was pulled down by Allan Adams and the timbers were reused.

'Eva Ayers and Norm Hubbard were married in this church. We all went to see the newlyweds. It was very exciting for us kids. A few nights later we gave them a tin-kettling, everyone walking down the road banging on pots and pans. I can still hear and see them in the dusk of the day.' Barbara Hunt Harris, 2011

Left to right: Bernie Hunt, Charlie Hunt, Molly Hunt, Lincoln Hunt, unknown, Normie Fryer.
Front row: Ted (Edward) Hunt, Auntie Fan Hunt, Lydia Hunt, Jean and Button Hunt.
(From the collection of Meryl Collinson)

(Courtesy of Yarra Glen & District Historical Society)

Mr Morris the teacher was also the postmaster. Quite against regulations, he set up the Steels Creek post office in an old washhouse that was stationed next door to the schoolroom. If anyone came to the post office during the day, Mr Morris would pop out to attend to them. One day an Education Department inspector visited and told him that he was breaking the rules. Easily fixed. The washhouse was moved a few metres to the other side of the fence. Charlie Bath would deliver the mail from Yarra Glen, and it would be sorted into pigeonholes and given to the children to take home. In time the phone line was wired into the shed and it became the telephone exchange. When another post office manager took over the position, the whole operation would be moved to a new location. This continued until the 1950s.

(Courtesy of Yarra Glen & District Historical Society)

(Courtesy of Yarra Glen & District Historical Society)

The original school building burnt down in 1943 and a new one was built in 1945. When it closed to students, the local community lobbied for ownership of it, to be used as a Community Centre. The shire purchased the property from the state government in 1992 and the building was made available to the community at no cost other than normal ongoing maintenance. It is deeply loved.

'On reflection I think that if the Centre had been lost [in the fires] I would probably have just given up. But to emerge from the devastation and to find the old school still there seemed to be a good reason to hold the morning tea [market] and try to rally together as many of us as possible. I never expected almost 200 people!' Keith Montell, *The Jolly Thing* (August–September 2010).

(Courtesy of Yarra Glen & District Historical Society)

(Courtesy of Yarra Glen & District Historical Society)

Fire

Tom Griffiths

In Steels Creek, elemental bushfire has swept up and down the valley several times every human generation and sometimes every few years. And its timber buildings have regularly been engulfed from the inside, by the escape of domestic flame. Hearth fire and bushfire have separate but entwining histories. 'Bushfire', as its name declares, came from outside, from the hills and the vegetation; it was an external force. But there was another kind of fire danger with which people lived every day, every season.

Hearth fire

Early Steels Creek, like most Australian rural communities before the Second World War, had a daily, familiar relationship with hearth fire – the camp fire, chimney fire, kitchen fire, candles and lamps that gave houses warmth, food and light. From the earliest days of white settlement, the camp fire was both solace and hazard. In 1869, two women friends of Steels Creek went shopping in Yarra Glen. There they drank a bit too much before walking towards home. Becoming tired they made a fire and lay down for the night. Ellen White awoke in flames with her clothes alight, and died later in hospital.[1] Reading, talking, singing and knitting were done by 'the yellow pleasure of candle-light' or the kerosene lamp.[2] Revellers at the Siggins' barn always arrived with lamps that were strung up for light and atmosphere. Outside, the night was very dark and the stars burned brightly: country towns scheduled evening meetings by the full moon. Bonfire Night was an annual celebration.

---

1   *Argus*, 26 June 1869, p. 5.
2   Blainey G (2003) *Black Kettle and Full Moon: Daily Life in a Vanished Australia*. Viking, Melbourne, p. 45.

Slab huts and timber dwellings gambled day and night with the fire at their heart. One child who grew up at a timber settlement near Big Pats Creek in the Warburton forest recalled that his home was made of rough timber, lined with hessian and covered with paper. Even the chimney was made of wood. 'Every night the fire had to be put out, followed by a good look up the chimney to see that it wasn't on fire.'[3] Maria Taylor's home at Dixons Creek had a wooden chimney until 1924, when it was replaced by a brick one. The fireplace 'seemed huge' – it had a ledge built around with bricks to keep the fire from burning the wood of the chimney, and children could sit on that ledge if the fire was small. Clothes hung there too, and over the fire itself were to be found iron kettles, boilers or billies, and usually a camp oven as well. Maria remembered one very cold evening when her father had put an extra large back log on the fire to keep it burning all night. In the early hours they awoke to a smell of burning and the discovery that the heavy timber at the base of the chimney was smouldering. A tragedy was averted.

In many homes, the last job of the last to bed was to 'bank the fire', to heap ash over the glowing coals so as to preserve them for the morning. 'Banking' referred to the mound of coals created but also to the investment made. Domestic fire was harboured and coddled, conjured and kindled. Sometimes it broke loose from this care. A log might roll from the fireplace while a woman was briefly outside; a curtain could waft over the candle in a child's bedroom; fat congealed on the kitchen stove might suddenly burst into flame.

In June 1904 the four-roomed home of Mr W. Friar of Steels Creek burned down. He had left home early in the evening, leaving a small fire burning in the grate. A few hours later he returned to find the place in flames. There was only a small insurance on the property and he had lost everything, including cash left in the house.[4] In April 1907, Mrs Brock of Steels Creek was baking and went outside to the paddock to tend her cows. While she was out, a spark probably caught on the wooden chimney, and soon the house was ablaze. Mrs Brock found that she was unable to fight the fire in the face of a stiff breeze: 'After having her fingers badly burnt, the poor old woman could only look at her house burning.' She lost everything, including a ton of potatoes. The house was uninsured and 'the poor old lady has only the clothes she stood in'.[5] In 1915, the home of Mr J. Hargreaves burned to the ground when he left a fire burning in the fireplace while he briefly visited his paddock. He, his wife and five young children were also left with nothing but the clothes they were wearing.[6] In November 1927, Jack and Agnes Walker were a little distance from their seven-roomed weatherboard home on Steels Creek Road when they saw smoke coming from one of the rooms. They were just in time to save their infant daughter from inside (a two-year-old who it is believed had been playing with a candle), but the house was totally destroyed.[7] The following year, Mr Kitchener's property was burnt down by a fire escaping from the fireplace when he was briefly absent. Nothing could be saved.[8] Violet Hunt's house burnt down because a log rolled out of the fire when she stepped out of the house, and Meryl Collinson's Auntie Mary's home was

3   'Horty's story', *Tirra Lirra*, Summer 1990–91, pp. 38–41, 59.

4   *Argus*, 11 June 1904, p. 6.

5   *Evelyn Observer and Bourke East Record*, 3 May 1907, p. 2.

6   *Healesville and Yarra Glen Guardian*, 3 July 1915; *Evelyn Observer*, 2 July 1915.

7   *Argus*, 2 November 1927, p. 15; information from Helen Mann.

8   *Advertiser* (Hurstbridge), 13 July 1928, p. 2.

destroyed when the radiator was too close to the curtains. The settlement's general store burnt down from the inside in the 1920s, but was soon replaced. It seldom paid to have a house burnt that was not insured, but the burning down of one old house in Steels Creek in 1898 – the decade of the valley's small mining boom – did result in the discovery of a hidden hoard of nearly 100 sovereigns.[9]

The Steels Creek School – a one-roomed weatherboard building on wooden stumps with a galvanised iron roof containing three hard-won cricket shields – was mysteriously destroyed by fire during the night of 2–3 June 1943. In winter it was usual for a fire to warm the schoolroom. On the afternoon of 2 June the fire was allowed to die out, and the teacher Miss Gwenneth Pitchford then removed the ashes as usual from the fireplace and placed them in a kerosene tin and poured water on the coals. That evening a very strong northerly wind blew up and perhaps it gusted down the chimney or penetrated the timbers and kindled some remnant embers back into life. Sometime during the night the building was alight with flame but no-one in the valley noticed until the teacher and pupils arrived the next morning to find a smoking ruin. A new school building – the one that remains today as the Community Centre – was first occupied two years later and officially opened in 1946.

Painting by Christine Mullen.

The burning of the Fletcher family home in February 1963 seemed the end of an era. It was 'one of the real pioneer homes and believed to be the first house built in Steels Creek', and it had miraculously survived many bushfires. But on Monday night it was standing and on Tuesday morning just a heap of charred rubble, the 'cause of the demise' again a mystery.

Houses were burnt down in Steels Creek, singly by domestic fire, almost as often as they were collectively engulfed by bushfire. And the two types of fire were related in intriguing ways. In the second half of the 20th century as domestic fire was expunged from daily life, bushfire gained in its capacity to surprise people who were less familiar with flame. The ubiquity of house fires had once reminded residents that houses were always vulnerable.

9   *Healesville and Yarra Glen Guardian*, 19 February 1898, p. 2.

Bushfires

There were bushfires every few summers in the Yarra Valley and there were great fires every few decades. The great fires were generally named – Black Thursday 1851, Red Tuesday 1898, Black Sunday 1926, the fires of 1932, Black Friday 1939, the fires of 1962, Ash Wednesday 1983 and Black Saturday 2009 – but fire on this scale also deserves a noun of its own. They were fires of a different order of magnitude to the normal summer fires; they could not be fought; they rampaged and killed. Let's call them 'firestorms', a word that has gained currency since Black Saturday that aptly describes their force and behaviour. All these firestorms visited the Steels Creek valley except for Ash Wednesday.

The memories of the firestorms – and the fact that they are noticed by the nation – can overwhelm the experience of regular, smaller, but still frightening and destructive fires that have been part of life in the valley. Thus the history of fire can sometimes obscure the reality of its own, normal ferocity. From the beginnings of European settlement at Steels Creek, there was a constant sense of summer peril. A conservative list of the summers when fire threatened or entered the valley looks like this: 1851, 1887, 1891, 1898, 1905, 1908, 1912, 1914, 1916, 1919, 1926, 1929, 1932, 1939, 1962, 1977, 1983, 2006 and 2009. And there have been more fires in the European history of Steels Creek than we know. In what follows, I will describe the bushfires and

William Strutt, Black Thursday, February 6th, 1851, *oil on canvas, 106.5 x 343.0 cm, 1864. (State Library of Victoria)*

firestorms together – in sequence and often drawing on the narratives of the time – so that we can see that they are all related and embedded in the rhythm of local life, and that they generated recurring language and imagery.

The great foundation fire of the colony of Victoria darkened the skies on 6 February 1851, known as Black Thursday. Temperatures reached 47°C, the sun seemed 'like a ball of red-hot iron', birds dropped dead from branches, 'pieces of flaming bark came whipping through the air', and all across Victoria – 'from the western coast to the Australian Alps, from the Snowy River to the Murray' – people fled and cowered before the 'most appalling roar' of the fires. As the visiting British writer and goldminer, William Howitt, put it: 'The whole country, for a time, was a furious furnace; and, what was most singular, *the greatest part of the mischief was done in a single day'.*[10] A thick fall of charred leaves fell on the beaches of northern Tasmania where the sea and sky of Bass Strait were 'black as night'.[11] For years the Yarra forests carried evidence of the firestorm. One traveller to the Upper Yarra in 1864 walked through 'one vast forest of dead trees, altogether destitute of bark or leaves; while the trunks and branches were bleached white with the weather'. He and his companions felt as if they were 'in a fog or mist'.[12]

Frederick Woodhouse, Fire and Flight, *wood engraving published in* The Australasian Sketcher, *20 February 1875. (State Library of Victoria)*

The summers of 1877–79 were bad fire seasons across Victoria and 10 years later, in January 1887, the Yarra Valley was experiencing a period of intense heat longer than any in 'the memory of the oldest inhabitant'. A fire was started at Holland's sawmill, Healesville, when a bullock driver used a red-hot iron to mend a bullock yoke and then dropped it on the ground when he had completed the job. Loose bark immediately ignited. Another fire began when three swagmen camped near Lilydale lit a fire against a log to boil their billies and neglected to put it out.[13] Other fires were on the loose in the forests, smoke enveloped the district for days, and residents were trying to beat the flames back from crops and homesteads. Buildings were destroyed and trees fell across roads. Splitters working the slopes of Mt St Leonard lost several months' stock of palings, all consumed by fire.[14] The *Lilydale Express* reported that the fires were so furious 'that on Tuesday the flames reached in some places to the tops of some of the highest trees in the forest'.[15]

10   McCrae GG (Spring 1989) Black Thursday, 6 February 1851. *La Trobe Library Journal* **11**(44), 20–21; Boldrewood R (1969) *Old Melbourne Memories.* William Heinemann, p. 118 and Howitt W (1855) *Land, Labour and Gold.* Boston, Vol. 2, pp. 190–191, quoted in Pyne SJ (1992) *Burning Bush: A Fire History of Australia.* Allen & Unwin, Sydney, pp. 221–222.

11   Fenton J (1970) *Bush Life in Tasmania Fifty Years Ago.* Originally published 1891, reprinted by Regal Publishers, Launceston, p. 80.

12   Anonymous, 'A visit to the Australian Alps' (condensed from an article in *Dicker's Mining Record*, April 1864). In: *Tracks to the Jordan.* (Ed. HJ Stacpoole) pp. 45–55. Lowden, Kilmore, 1973.

13   *Lilydale Express*, 14 & 21 January 1887.

14   *Lilydale Express*, 14 & 21 January 1887.

15   *Lilydale Express*, 11 February 1887.

In 1891, a surviving fragment of the diary of Steels Creek schoolteacher, Mr E.C. Morris, records the forbidding normality of fire in the valley:

9 Feb: It has been a horrible hot windy day, thermometer 92. …
         Bushfires are raging.
5 March: Fire started today out in Bell's paddock.
6 Mar: Fire burning fiercely today. Excessively hot again 95.
8 Mar: Warm again. Bushfire raging above Hunt's paddock.
         A few drops of rain checked it.[16]

In 1898 'Red Tuesday', worst in Gippsland, was the culmination of several hot summers and was a constellation of fires lit mostly by settlers wanting to rid their land of trees. On Tuesday 8 February (a week after 'Red Tuesday'), the north wind brought a fire 'which had been burning for several days in the mountains' right down Steels Creek, sweeping fences and grass before it. 'It was with great difficulty that the homes of the residents, as well as the State School and the Church of England, were saved.' Mr Jewson (senior) lost all he possessed. 'There were miles and miles of fencing destroyed, and hundreds of acres of grass as well. Some of the dairy farmers have no grass at all.'[17] The Steels Creek bridge was burnt down that summer.[18]

The homestead saved – An incident of the Great Gippsland Fire of 1898, *Globe Engraving Company, Melbourne, supplement to* The Australasian, *19 December 1908. (State Library of Victoria)*

There were major fires in Victoria almost every summer of the new century. In January 1905, fires raged at Steels Creek and Dixons Creek and the ranges beyond. Sawmills had narrow escapes and farmers again mourned the loss of grass and fencing, one losing '500 acres of grass and about 5 miles of fencing'. It was reported that: 'All the country from Kinglake to Steels Creek is one black mess.'[19]

16   Morris, E (1891), A year in the life of Edward Morris, Steels Creek, from his diary of 1891. Typescript in the Steels Creek Community Archive.
17   *Healesville and Yarra Glen Guardian*, 12 February 1898, p. 3.
18   *Healesville and Yarra Glen Guardian*, 12 October 1900, p. 3
19   *Healesville and Yarra Glen Guardian*, 21 January 1905, p. 2.

Three years later, in 1908, a bush fire at Toolangi burnt a large tract of country from the ridges down into the valley and destroyed every building on Mr Gordon's farm, including the cheese factory. Another fire burnt one of Steels Creek's admired fern gullies and 'did not stop until all the country to Yea had been traversed, when rain began to fall'.[20]

In 1912, bushfires again raged in Steels Creek and Christmas Hills, 'causing such intense excitement and anxiety'. Kilometres of country were burnt and much fencing destroyed. 'Christmas Hills and Steels Creek present a ruined blackened appearance, which is very visible since the heavy rain'. A very large fire had been burning at the head of Steels Creek, and 'had the hot weather continued, grave fears were entertained for the safety of several homesteads'.[21]

In February 1914, bushfires were burning on the hills for several days and on Friday 21 February a north-easterly gale blew the fire down from Kinglake into Steels Creek 'with a vengeance'. About 25 kilometres of country were burnt, 'and great difficulty was experienced in saving many houses'. The local men met and fought the fire at the top end of the valley and saved houses, but it then swept on down the creek. Word was sent to Yarra Glen for help, 'but there were no men available', although several from Dixons Creek gave assistance. Fences and grass again were lost. The roadside was strewn with trees grubbed for removal and they fed the fire.[22] The creek did not start to run again until late April.[23]

Two years later, in February 1916, bushfires on the ranges were 'very bad'. A Bush Fire Brigade was formed that summer in Yarra Glen. Mr Morris sent two men to put out burning logs and debris after an earlier fire was doused by rain, and the *Evelyn Observer* reported that 'If it had not been done, well, I think we would have had a bad time of it.'[24]

In early February 1919, as another dry season strengthened, smoke from bush fires enveloped the valley, visibility was poor, 'the sun shone with a brownish tint, and the leaves glistened like burnished copper'. A bushfire broke out of the range at the head of Steels Creek and burnt out many paddocks and much fencing. Many of the settlers' houses were threatened but local firefighters managed to protect them.[25]

Men fighting bushfires in Australia, *c. 1940s. (Argus Newspaper Collection of Photographs, State Library of Victoria)*

20   *Sydney Morning Herald*, 11 March 1908; *Evelyn Observer*, 20 March 1908.

21   *Healesville and Yarra Glen Guardian*, 9 February 1912, p. 2.

22   *Evelyn Observer and Bourke East Record*, 27 February 1914, p. 3.

23   *Healesville and Yarra Glen Guardian*, 24 April 1915, p. 3.

24   *Evelyn Observer and Bourke East Record*, 4 February 1916, p. 2.

25   *Argus*, 5 February 1919, p. 5; *Healesville and Yarra Glen Guardian*, 8 February 1919, p. 2.

In these first decades of the 20th century, the frequency of major fires quickened as more people were living and working in dangerous environments. Sawmilling had moved deeper into the forests, expanding from the slower-growing, more durable eucalyptus species of the foothill forests into the tall, even-aged stands of the mountain ash. Steam-powered winches made the steep ash forests millable and the development of a seasoning process in the 1920s enabled mountain ash (which was inclined otherwise to warp) to become Melbourne's most popular building timber. Small, isolated communities were established in the wet sclerophyll forests: a substantial sawmill settlement might have a tennis court, school and even a football team, and some women escaped to town only a couple of times a year. The fragile lifelines of the bush communities were the narrow timber tramways that brought the sawn timber to the railheads. It was a deadly predicament. In the Steels Creek valley sawmilling also pushed further into the ranges but the men returned home at the end of the day.

The 1926 firestorm – Black Sunday – was terrifying: 'the worst tragedy that has been experienced in Victoria since the recent war'. The bushfires, declared the *Lilydale Express*, were 'abnormal'. The fire 'thundered'; it was 'a grim demon'; 'the roar of it was tremendous'; it 'came over in a cyclonic manner'. 'The spectacle of the roaring sea of fire mounting up hundreds of feet will not soon be forgotten', reported the *Healesville Guardian*. Although named for a day, the 1926 fires rampaged for six weeks and took 60 lives across Victoria, many of them in those isolated sawmill settlements. The clanging of fire bells was constant in the Yarra Ranges that summer, smoke hung ominously in the air for weeks, and hundreds of firefighters surged to the latest outbreak. In Healesville, householders were asked to turn off their taps when the fire bell rang so that water pressure might be strengthened. If the worst day had not been a Sunday, there would have been many more deaths of bush workers. Such was the ferocity of the fire that bodies were extremely difficult to identify.[26]

From mid-February that year, Steels Creek was threatened by the bushfires surrounding it and bush residents were in a constant state of anxiety. Outbreaks of fire near Queenstown and Kinglake converged in one large stream of flame 'and poured down into Steels Creek' on the night of Black Sunday, 14 February 1926. For the next few days firefighters were working day and night to control the flames and the homes of the Hubbard and Morris families were saved. The western side of Steels Creek road was burned. A week later a north wind, accompanied by a thundering roar, drove 'leaping flames through the tree tops' and the town of Kinglake was reduced to smouldering heaps of ash. That same night, 24 February, fires encircled Dixons Creek and flaming bark from trees on the ridge above were blown into the settlement. The Methodist Church and three houses were destroyed. Two days later, fire again threatened the whole valley, but was brought under control with help from the men of Steels Creek and Yarra Glen.[27]

---

26   *Lilydale Express*, 5 February 1926, p. 3; 12 February 1926, p. 1; 19 February 1926, p. 3; 5 March 1926, p. 2.

27   *Argus*, 20 February 1926, 10 March 1926, p. 21; *Healesville and Yarra Glen Guardian*, 6 February 1926, p. 1; 20 February 1926, pp. 1–2; 27 February 1926, p. 3.

Allan Adams was seven when the 1926 fire came through and he remembered how the Country Roads Board men working on the Mt Slide Road came down and cut a firebreak around his place 'and come about midnight they burnt back towards the fire and that saved us, because we had no way of getting out, no transport or anything'. Doreen Ayres (née Hubbard) recalled how the school beach picnic was generally in February but 'Dad never ever went' because of the bush fire danger. And sure enough, in 1926, 'we came home [and] the hills were all alight'. She remembers making the terrible mistake of walking to Kinglake on 24 February to see if her friend's family were all right, and she found the Kinglake Hotel on fire. 'Silly thing to do, you know, you do stupid things!'[28]

In February 1929, just as the Steels Creek 'ladies' cricket match' was about to commence, a telephone message was received in the little post office saying that a fire had broken out on top of the Quarry Hill, on the Steels Creek road. Two carloads of volunteers rushed to the spot, and with help from some Yarra Glen men they soon had the fire under control. About 15 acres of grass were burnt and several fence posts.[29]

The 1932 fire was 1926 all over again, burning the same places and once more taking lives. Bushfires raged in the region for a fortnight and again the newspapers searched for words with which to describe another abnormal fire that was beginning to seem normal: 'Man's arch enemy, the fire fiend, obtained a relentless grip upon the district … It was obvious that nothing

could stay its advance, as the wind was blowing like a hurricane. There was no time to do anything before, with a roar like thunder, the fire swept into the valley. In places it was a perfect wall of flame, while burning leaves and bark were falling in a shower of fire all round. Houses caught and burnt like waste paper. … the flames reached tremendous proportions … It was only a matter of minutes from the time the flames were seen until they were flung upon the township [Warburton], through which it swept, burning everything. Except for the loss of life it is considered to be even worse than the fire of six years ago.' It left the earth 'as bare and as black as a coal mine'.[30]

But these recurrent, intensifying firestorms that savaged the isolated bush communities and terrorised the towns of the Yarra Ranges were just a preamble, just a series of opening acts, to the fires of 1939, Black Friday. Intensive logging had allowed masses of dead and drying treetops to build up on the forest floor. That summer season was searingly hot and it followed a long dry winter. The prolonged drought had left creeks running at record lows or not running at all, and the bush crackled ominously under the boots of bush workers. Maria Taylor recalled that in 1939 the bush was so tinder dry that 'the boys were afraid to wear their heavy boots outside, in case the nails in the soles should ignite the grass as they walked'. Frank Gibson, who later moved to Steels Creek, had 55 acres at Warranwood near Warrandyte and on the morning of Black Friday he put the thermometer outside (it climbed to 114.5°F the last time he was able to look) and he was constantly sniffing the air not just for smoke (which was everywhere) but 'for *fresh* smoke'.[31]

28   Ayres D, Conversation with Helen and Tim Todhunter.
29   *Advertiser* (Hurstbridge), 1 March 1929.
30   *Lilydale Express*, 22 January 1932, p. 3; 12 February 1932, p. 1.
31   Frank Gibson, letter to his brother-in-law John, 11 June 1939, Yarra Glen and District Historical Society, brought to our attention by Helen Mann.

Fire fighting in 1939. (Department of Primary Industries, Victoria)

Black Friday was Friday, 13 January, and it was the grim climax of a week of horror. In that week, 1.4 million hectares of Victoria burned, whole settlements were incinerated, and 71 people died. Sixty-nine timber mills were engulfed, 'steel girders and machinery were twisted by heat as if they had been of fine wire', and the whole state seemed to be alight.[32] Judge Leonard Stretton who presided over the Royal Commission into the causes of the fires captured their power in words that would echo down the years:

The speed of the fires was appalling. They leaped from mountain peak to mountain peak, or far out into the lower country, lighting the forests 6 or 7 miles in advance of the main fires. Blown by a wind of great force, they roared as they travelled. Balls of crackling fire sped at a great pace in advance of the fires, consuming with a roaring, explosive noise, all that they touched.

Houses of brick were seen and heard to leap into a roar of flame before the fires had reached them. Some men of science hold the view that the fires generated and were preceded by inflammable gases which became alight. Great pieces of burning bark were carried by the wind to set in raging flame regions not yet reached by the fires.

Such was the force of the wind that, in many places, hundreds of trees of great size were blown clear of the earth, tons of soil, with embedded masses of rock, still adhering to the roots; for mile upon mile the former forest monarchs were laid in confusion, burnt, torn from the earth, and piled one upon another as matches strewn by a giant hand.

Judge Stretton also had words to describe the predicament of those living and working in the bush:

Men who had lived their lives in the bush went their ways in the shadow of dread expectancy. But though they felt the imminence of danger they could not tell that it was to be far greater than they could imagine. They had not lived long enough. The experience of the past could not guide them to an understanding of what might, and did, happen.

32   Stretton LEB (1939) *Report of the Royal Commission into the causes of and measures taken to prevent the bushfires of January 1939.* Government Printer, Melbourne, p. 1.

Stretton was not commenting on the youthfulness of the dead: he was lamenting the environmental knowledge of both victims and survivors. He was pitying the innocence of European immigrants in a land whose natural rhythms they did not yet understand. He was depicting the fragility and brevity of a human lifetime in forests where life cycles and fire regimes had the periodicity and ferocity of centuries.

People spoke disbelievingly of the deafening roar and blasting wind of the firestorm, the tornadoes that ripped trees off at ground level, the explosions of gas, the fireballs, the instant combustion of buildings, the streamers of bark dropping into valleys, the flames leaping kilometres ahead. There was the vulnerable innocence of those who did not know the scale of what they were fighting until it was too late. There was the machinery at bush sawmills that

George Sellars, the lone survivor of the 1939 fire at Fitzpatrick's Mill in the Matlock Forest. (From Bush fires: A pictorial survey of Victoria's most tragic week, January 8-15, 1939, *Sun News-Pictorial, Melbourne)*

Blackened trees line Blacks Spur Road between Healesville and Marysville, 1939. (Department of Primary Industries, Victoria)

became a molten mess. There was the dead silence of the day after, with not a bird or animal or leaf to stir, and the creeks running black as ink. And just as there had been after 1851, there was the mist that seemed for years after 1939 to hang low over the Yarra Ranges, a mist made up of bleached, dead spars, the skeletons of the former forest.[33]

The Steels Creek valley was caught up in a national tragedy, 'the most disastrous forest calamity the State of Victoria had known'. Christmas Hills, Steels Creek and Yarra Glen were 'encompassed by a holocaust'. For the whole week residents had anxiously followed the drama in other towns and forests, and then suddenly found their own valley attacked from two directions. A fire thought to have been started at Queenstown near St Andrews was 'lashed into action by a north-westerly gale that reached a velocity of about 60 miles an hour'. It 'literally swept over the countryside, leaving a catastrophic trail of ruin'. People sheltered in a mining tunnel and firefighters fought the flames on both sides of the Steels Creek road. Captain W.J. Dickens lost his home there and all the buildings on his farm, and as the fire swept towards his property, 'his wife and two children had to run for shelter near a creek.'[34] Then word came from Yarra Glen that the town was in danger and most of the fighters rushed to save the Memorial Hall which was being licked by flame. By a little after noon, Yarra Glen was a raging furnace, and the situation seemed so perilous that many of the women and children had evacuated the town. Although firefighters saved many buildings, 31 homes were destroyed in the Yarra Glen–Steels Creek district, including the humble bark hut of 'Old Man Riddell' on the edge of Kinglake National Park. And the Dixons Creek Methodist church was burnt down again.

Sawmill employees carrying victims after Black Friday 1939. (Department of Primary Industries, Victoria).

There were survivors and heroes. Nellie Hunt – 'Auntie Nellie' to everyone – barricaded herself in her little house and refused to be evacuated, and so Bill Adams and one of his older brothers had to force entry to her home so that they could take her to safety. Gordon Hubbard drove his motor car again and again into the heart of the fires, ferrying women and children to safer ground. Barbara Hunt Harris recalled that, on that day, she and others were being given a lift by Alf Adams when they had to stop and change a tyre as the fire approached. 'You could hear the fire roaring over the side of the mountain.' Then Gordon Hubbard miraculously appeared and drove them out. They lay

33   Ogden M (n.d.) *My life in the forests of Victoria and the timber industry (1914–1976)*. Unpublished typescript, Melbourne, p. 133, Department of Primary Industries Library. Part of this account has been published in Dargavel J (1988) *Sawing, Selling and Sons: Histories of Australian Timber Firms*. Centre for Resource and Environmental Studies, Australian National University, Canberra, pp. 93–99.

34   *Argus*, 16 January 1939, p. 2.

in a ploughed paddock during the fire. Barbara remembered how the fire burnt through the Yarra Glen cemetery, and their companion, 'Old Mrs Jell', cried as she watched it scour the graves. When the little party finally reached home, they slept outside and the hills were burning around them all through the night. Along Steels Creek road, two men who escaped from a burning home then sheltered in a water tank, but as that became too hot, they fled to another house which they also had to abandon as flames took hold of it. The bush was alight all around them. At that moment, Gordon Hubbard appeared and managed to rescue the two trapped men and take them to Yarra Glen.[35] He did this, according to the *Healesville and Yarra Glen Guardian*, 'by what is now regarded as supernatural means'.

In January 1962, the people of Steels Creek and especially of the Dandenongs feared that 1939 was happening all over again. On Sunday 14 January 1962, five major bushfires broke out in the Dandenongs and in the mountains surrounding Yarra Glen and Healesville. For three terrible days, the entire district from Ferntree Gully on the far slope of the Dandenongs to Healesville and Warburton, was threatened 'by an inferno which equalled in ferocity the never-to-be-forgotten bush-fires which engulfed the same areas 23 years ago, on Black Friday, January 13, 1939'. More than 400 homes were burnt, eight lives lost and many thousands of cattle, sheep and household pets killed. 'Mile after mile … was reduced to black ruin', declared the *Lilydale Express*, echoing Judge Stretton's description of 1939.[36]

At Christmas Hills on the Sunday afternoon, 14 January, two men – described in the local press as 'strangers to the district' – were endeavouring to smoke a ferret from a rabbit hole when the fire got away from them and burned towards Yarra Glen. On Tuesday another change of wind fanned the fire into fresh fury and swept it in a northerly direction 'with a trainlike roar' towards Steels Creek.[37] Just before it reached the settlement it branched along the old Kinglake Road from where it swept into the Kinglake National Park and on to St Andrews. Dozens of the Steels Creek farm properties on both sides of the road were threatened, but firefighters saved the houses. A relief depot was established in the Yarra Glen Memorial Hall where women sent out sandwiches and water with lemon to the fire fronts and bathed the eyes of returning men.[38] Evelyn Smith of Yarra Glen didn't see her husband or boys for four days: her Sunday roast was cooking when the fire started and it was never eaten. Welcome rain fell soon after midnight on Tuesday. Residents of the valley felt that a tragedy the scale of 1939 had been narrowly averted.

As the fire bears down upon you, what kind of treasures do you gather together and run outside with? One lady in the Dandenongs evacuated into the middle of a potato patch with the photo miniatures of her children, two small Chinese carved ivory dogs and her two best pairs of cutting-out scissors. Fine scissors were widely treasured. Her friend took two cookery books, a dictionary, an old black 'Dinah Doll', a pair of snow boots, a special Belgian parsley cutter, some knitting needles and a fruitcake. One of the cookery

---

35   *Healesville and Yarra Glen Guardian*, 21 January 1939; *Advertiser* (Hurstbridge), 20 January 1939, p. 5, and information from Barbara Hunt Harris and Meryl Collinson.

36   *Lilydale Express*, Friday 19 January 1962.

37   Howden M (1999) *Community Life in Yarra Glen: Evelyn Smith's Story*. Mary Howden, Melbourne.

38   *Lilydale Express*, 19 January 1962.

books was an autobiography by the English restaurant critic, Fanny Cradock, called *Something's Burning*.[39]

A child living in the vicarage at Croydon in Melbourne's eastern suburbs remembers waking on a strange, dark day in January to see a long line of women evacuated from Kalorama to the church hall, waiting to use the garden tap, while her mother was in the kitchen cooking 70 boiled eggs. Her father, the vicar, eventually arrived home with his eyebrows singed. Too young to serve in the Second World War, the battle against fire in the nearby hills became 'his war'.[40]

The 1962 fire, with its heart in the Dandenongs so close to the expanding suburbs of Melbourne, signalled a new type of bushfire in Australian history. The bush had come to town. But the town had also come to the bush, insinuating its commuters and their homes among the gums. The 1962 fire anticipated other dramatic fires of this growing urban interface with the bush: Black Tuesday (Hobart) 1967, Ash Wednesday 1983, Sydney 1994, Canberra 2003 and Black Saturday 2009.

When Steels Creek residents gathered at their Community Centre in 1996 to hear the beloved former schoolteacher, Vera Adams, talk about local history, the main fire that was recalled – but only just and only by some – was 1962. Vera remembered how the 1962 fire had burnt along the back fences of properties on the west side of Steels Creek Road and had just missed the school. She had been holidaying with her sons in a caravan at Rosebud at the time. At

a Teachers' Conference several weeks after the fire Vera heard the Christmas Hills teacher, Peter Evenden, remark on the progress of his school's new septic toilet construction. Vera wanted to know why the Christmas Hills School, with similar enrolments to Steels Creek, had been so favoured by the Education Department. 'Well,' explained Peter, 'I was there on the scene when the fire came through.' 'And you were able to save the toilets?' asked Vera. 'I was able to persuade the firefighters to take a break', he answered. It was a few more years before the primitive outhouses of the Steels Creek School were replaced.

At least two fires threatened Steels Creek in the 1970s, a burn-off from the Kinglake National Park and another that came close to the school.[41] The Ash Wednesday firestorm of 1983 spared the settlement, although just two days before it rampaged, a small fire had broken out in the National Park above the valley and had been successfully controlled. There were other smaller fires in the final decades of the 20th century and one that threatened from the ridge and was controlled in 2006, but it was the 1962 fire, and before that 1939, that continued to carry forward the local, barely remembered experience of a firestorm in Steels Creek. As the drought deepened in the valley in the first decade of the 21st century, those years seemed long ago.

Burning off

The British colonists of Australia came from a land without a well-defined fire season where fire had been suppressed and domesticated over generations, from a countryside that was relatively free of wild fire. They had so tamed fire that they had literally internalised it in the 'internal combustion' of the steam

---

39   *Lilydale Express*, 2 February 1962.

40   Information from Libby Robin and Mrs Elizabeth Robin.

41   Garey J (n.d.) Memories of Steels Creek 1972–1982. Steels Creek Community Archive.

engine. These representatives of the industrial revolution brought to Australia many new sources of ignition, yet the colonists also introduced houses, cattle, sheep, fences and all kinds of material belongings that made them fear wild fire. And they found themselves in a land that nature and human culture had sculpted with fire over millennia, a land that was hungry for fire, and a land widowed of its stewards by the European invasion. It was an explosive combination.

Mary Gilmore, growing up in the NSW Riverina, vividly recalled her family's stories of that cultural education in fire:

> My grandparents used to tell of how new immigrants when they first came to the country, unaccustomed to the danger in the wild country, would start fires and let them run heedless of the result; and then stand panic-stricken at having loosed something they could not control. And they would go on to relate how the natives would run for bushes, put them into the immigrants' hands, and show them how to beat back the flame as it licked up the grass. Indeed it was a constant wonder, when I was little, how easily the blacks would check a fire before it grew too big for close handling, or start a return fire when and where it was safest.[42]

Settlers feared and suppressed fire near their properties and towns, and misjudged its power in the bush. But it did not take them long to begin to use fire for their own purposes, even if clumsily and dangerously. In 1855 the visiting English writer William Howitt described the Victorian gold rush

The Morning After the Fire, *wood engraving published in* The Illustrated Australian News and Musical Times, *1 April 1890. (State Library of Victoria)*

populace as 'this fire scattering race of rude men'. The diggers, he said, 'burn up the country wherever they go, as they say, to get rid of snakes.'[43] 'The whole Australian race', declared one bushman, has 'a weakness for burning.'[44] The language the bush workers used – 'burning to clean up the country' – was uncannily like that of Aboriginal people.

Fire had been one of the weapons with which Aboriginal people fought the invaders of their land and soon the invaders themselves were using it to prospect, clear, farm and graze. And occasionally they, too, used it as a

42   Gilmore M (1986) *Old Days Old Ways: A Book of Recollections*. Angus & Robertson, Sydney, first published 1934, 1986 illustrated edition, p. 185.

43   Pyne SJ, *Burning Bush*, p. 196.

44   Noble WS (1973) *Ordeal by Fire*. Hawthorn Press, Melbourne, p. 10.

weapon. Swagmen who were denied a job at a homestead might use the threat of fire as a punishment. One squatter who refused to employ a traveller as a shepherd explained why by pointing to his new brush fence, saying, 'That is my shepherd.' 'Oh!' replied the swagman, shaking a box of matches, 'if that's your shepherd, here is his ---- master.'[45] Arson remains a significant and disturbing form of social protest.

The imperative for settlers was to 'improve' the land they had colonised, and 'improvement' first meant clearing. The Australian settler or 'pioneer' was a heroic figure depicted as battling the land and especially the trees. A witness to the Royal Commission inquiring into the 1939 fires explained that:

After the gold rush was over, the white man had to make use of the land and he had to get rid of the timber. He slaved, toiled and burned to get rid of it. … The children and grandchildren of these men have grown up with minds opposed to timber.[46]

Settlers were often overwhelmed and frustrated by the quantity of bush timber, and clearing it was seen not only as a private necessity but also as a public good. William Howitt erroneously referred to Australia as 'one huge, reclaimed forest' which he believed was unhealthy due to the mass of uncleared vegetable matter it generated. 'All these evils', he wrote, 'the axe and the plough, and the fire of settlers, will gradually and eventually remove.'[47]

These were indeed the instruments of destruction. One selector in eastern Victoria estimated that, in the first five to ten years on the land, nine-tenths of the labour was devoted to axe-work.[48]

This fight with the forest assumed theatrical dimensions in South Gippsland, where each summer neighbours gathered to watch the giant burns that, they hoped, would turn last year's fallen and ring-barked forest into this year's clearing. They needed to establish pastures as quickly and cheaply as possible. Small trees were chopped, undergrowth was slashed, and sometimes large trees were felled so as to demolish smaller timber that had been previously 'nicked', thereby creating 'a vast, crashing, smashing, splintering, roaring and thundering avalanche of falling timber!'[49] The slashed forest was left to dry until the weather was hot enough for the annual burn, the frightening climax of the pioneer's year. In the mostly wet sclerophyll forest of the South Gippsland ranges, some of it mountain ash, it was often hard to get a 'good

Fighting the fire, *wood engraving published in the Supplement to* The Australasian Sketcher, *8 April 1885.* (State Library of Victoria)

45   Crombie A (1927) *After Sixty Years or Recollections of an Australian Bushman*. Watson, Ferguson & Co. Ltd, Brisbane, p. 31.

46   Quoted in Noble WS, *Ordeal by Fire*, pp. 10–11.

47   Quoted in Bolton G (1981) *Spoils and Spoilers: Australians Make their Environment, 1788–1980*. Allen & Unwin, Sydney, p. 41.

48   South Gippsland Development League (1920) *The Land of the Lyrebird: A Story of Early Settlement in the Great Forest of South Gippsland*. Shire of Korumburra, Korumburra, p. 54.

49   *The Land of the Lyrebird*, p. 59.

burn' because of the heavy rainfall and the inability of wind to penetrate the thick scrub.[50] Farmers therefore chose the hottest summer days for these burns, 'the windier and hotter the day the better for our purpose'. These settlers of the world's most fire-prone forests awaited the most fatal days. They were unwittingly re-creating the natural process that had produced and sustained the very forests they wanted to destroy. And so the forest fought back with unexpected vigour and secondary clearance greatly increased the cost of farm establishment and, in perhaps a third of cases, led to the abandonment of properties.[51]

The annual burn was 'a spectacle that for awful grandeur beggars description': everything was tinged with 'that weird, eerie, livid, yellowish-green hue … the face of the sun appearing like a great dull copper disc'.[52] It was a time of great unease and irritability as well as excitement, as residents breathed their neighbours' smoke and anxiously watched the wind direction.[53] Laboriously constructed split rail fences, homes and, sometimes, human lives were lost in the cause of clearing. After a good burn logs were picked up and fired a second time to clear the ground. 'What a change two hours of fire had wrought! We were forest dwellers no longer', exclaimed one selector. W.M. Elliot rejoiced that 'not a vestige remains of the vast forest that once so stubbornly resisted our labours. Hill and vale covered in verdure as far as the

eye can see!'[54] A 'good burn' could so easily become a wildfire and on Red Tuesday 1898 it did. That fire was the ultimate pioneering weapon run amok. It only accelerated the pace of settlement.[55]

In the drier forests of the ranges (but generally not the wet mountain ash forests which had less grass), graziers used fire as Aboriginal people had done: to keep the forest open, to clean up the scrub, to encourage a 'green pick', and to protect themselves and their stock from dangerous bushfire. But, unlike Aboriginal people, some were prepared to burn in any season. In 1887, the *Lilydale Express* felt the need to remind its readers that, even when the weather turned cooler, 'there should be some caution used in setting the bush on fire'. In the first decades of the 20th century, when travelling in the Yarra Valley, it was normal to see 'half a dozen fires on the sides of mountains'.[56]

Steels Creek residents were as keen on burning off as anyone. Barbara Rolfe always had a box of matches in her pocket as she walked around, ready to light the bush to bring on a green pick for her cows. In the hot February of 1891 as Edward Morris recorded threatening bushfires in his diary, he was also burning rubbish on his property: '23 Feb: Just been lighting some of my heaps. 24 Feb: Burned a few more heaps this afternoon.' Two months later, William Hubbard was doing a bit of burning off by the creek but 'owing to the

50   Swaffield JB (1972) Back to Neerim history. Quoted in: *Warragul and District Historical Society Monthly Bulletin* no. 48, 17 April.
51   Frost W (1998) European farming, Australian pests: agricultural settlement and environmental disruption in Australia, 1800–1920. *Environment and History* **4**(2), 135–136.
52   Quoted in Dingle AE (1984) *Settling. Volume 2 of The Victorians*. Fairfax, Syme & Weldon Associates, Melbourne, p. 67.
53   McLeary A with Dingle T (1998) *Catherine: On Catherine Currie's Diary, 1873–1908*. Melbourne University Press, Melbourne, pp. 54, 77–78.
54   Dingle AE, *Settling*, p. 67.
55   Pyne SJ, *Burning Bush*, pp. 240–244.
56   'Transcript of evidence given before the Royal Commission to enquire into the causes and origins and other matters arising out of bush fires in Victoria during the month of January 1939'. Three volumes. Victorian Government, Melbourne, 1939 (Department of Primary Industries Library, Melbourne), p. 79.

heat of the sun and the hot wind' the fire got away and rapidly spread through the rushes and dry timber. 'After burning for about an hour and a half it was checked by the kind assistance of the neighbours before it did any damage, except the destruction of about 30 acres of grass.'[57]

In 1939, the Royal Commission into the Black Friday bushfires investigated the settlers' culture of burning. Judge Stretton's shocking finding was that 'These fires were lit by the hand of man.'[58] Stretton highlighted 'the indifference with which forest fires, as a menace to the interests of all, have been regarded'. Fire was someone else's responsibility. It was, as one witness to the commission put it, 'nobody's business to put out'. And who were the firebugs? Rarely were they malevolent arsonists. Mostly they were farmers and bush workers, and their fire lighting was sometimes casual and selfish, sometimes systematic and sensible, and increasingly clandestine and rebellious. They were ordinary people going about their lives who liked fire and were careless of its consequences, or who feared wildfire and wanted to pre-empt it. They were settlers burning to clear land, graziers firing the grass to promote new growth, miners blazing a path to a new reef, jackeroos signalling their whereabouts to their bosses. Burning was a rite – and a right. They were homeowners who, when they saw smoke on the horizon, threw a match over the back fence.

In the 1920s and 1930s in the Yarra Valley, there was an ongoing fight between settlers and foresters about the wisest use of fire and each saw the firestorms of 1926, 1932 and 1939 as products of the other's malpractice. Settlers indulged in 'burning off' and felt it helped to keep them and their neighbours safe. Forest officers, charged with conservation of timber, tried to suppress fire. Jack Ezard, a renowned sawmiller, acknowledged that lighting a fire at the wrong time could be a criminal act, but he also insisted that 'I think it is almost as criminal an act not to light a fire at the right time.'[59] George Purvis, a storekeeper and grazier at Moe in Gippsland explained to the 1939 Royal Commission that the forest officers were 'so keen that they hate to see even a little gum tree destroyed and that is where we think differently from them'. Everybody used to burn off many years ago, he explained: 'We could meet a few of our neighbours and say "What about a fire" … Nowadays, if we want a fire we nick out in the dark, light it, and let it go. We are afraid to tell even our next door neighbour because the Forests Commission is so definitely opposed to fires anywhere, that we are afraid to admit that we have anything to do with them.' As a result, he explained, the bulk of farmers did not burn their land as much as they wished. And so, as fires gathered force in the week before Black Friday, people desperately burnt to save their property and their lives – it was considered better to burn late than never – and these fires (indeed 'lit by the hand of man') 'went back into the forest where they all met in one huge fire'.

Perhaps fire was so much a part of the Australian landscape and character that it could never be eliminated or suppressed. It had to be accepted and used, and perhaps it could be controlled. Stretton was not the first to condemn Australian carelessness with fire: he joined a long tradition. In 1890 George Perrin, Victoria's first Conservator of Forests, described the 'universal carelessness with regard to fire' as 'culpable negligence', and annual reports of the Victorian Forests Department and later Forests Commission echoed

57   *Evelyn Observer*, 2 April 1891.
58   Stretton LEB, *Report of the Royal Commission*, 1939, p. 5.
59   'Transcript of evidence given before the Royal Commission' (1939), pp. 26, 30.

these words.[60] However, the 1939 Royal Commission signalled a new direction. It gave official recognition to a folk reality and tried to give direction and discipline to the widespread popular practice of burning to keep the forest safe. It recommended that the best protection against fire was regular light burning of undergrowth at times other than summer. Only fire could beat fire.

It took time for official 'controlled burning' to supplant unofficial 'burning off'. The 1962 fires, like 1939, were 'man-made', as the newspapers put it, mostly deliberately lit, not by 'arsonists' but by settlers hoping to manage and protect their land. A further dramatic example of the persistence of rural traditions of burning was the 1967 Hobart fire (another Black Tuesday, another 7 February), which caused the largest loss of life and property on any single day in Australia to that time. It had strong elements of 1939 embedded within it. Of the 110 fires burning on that Tuesday, 90 started prior to the day and 70 were uncontrolled on the morning of 7 February. A further stunning fact: only 22 of the 110 fires were started accidentally; 88 were deliberately lit. In other words, bushfires were common, deliberate and were allowed to burn unchecked. 'No-one worried about them too much', reflected fire officer, John Gledhill, 40 years later.

During the second half of the 20th century, casual rural fire lighting gradually became criminal. The law was enforced more strongly and public acceptance of open flame declined. As well as the farming tradition of 'burning off', there was the problem of city people coming to the bush for recreational fire. Picnicking

and 'boiling the billy' were the major ways that city folk interacted with the bush. Australians are the great tea-drinkers of the world and there has always been something mystically patriotic in firing up the billy and stirring in the tea-leaves with a gum twig. As Geoffrey Blainey put it, 'Firewood was so plentiful that boiling the billy was as common in Australia as it was uncommon in Europe.'[61] But, as reported by the Lilydale Express when anticipating the fire season in the hot January of 1962, 'It seems a pity that a few people cannot enjoy themselves in our bushlands and countryside without resorting to the lighting of fires.'[62] The Chief Officer at the CFA, A.W. Larkins, distinguished between 'essential' and 'unessential' fires. Some people still needed open fires for cooking and washing, so it was difficult to police fairly. 'The worst offenders', noted the newspaper, 'are city and townspeople who, when in the country, light fires in the vicinity of properties where the fire-conscious country people will not even allow the general smoking of cigarettes during the dangerous summer months.'[63]

Following 1939 there were greater efforts to prosecute for careless fire lighting. In March 1940 a Steels Creek farmer was fined for having lit fires during a prohibited period and in a prohibited area. When the policeman commented 'I see you have been doing a bit of burning off?', the farmer replied: 'I thought this was a free country. I might as well be at the war.' The conviction was quashed on appeal because there was no certainty about who lit the fires. In 1944 a Steels Creek resident was fined 10 pounds for lighting 31 fires on his property when burning off logs and ferns in January.[64]

60   Perrin G (1890) Report of the Conservator of Forests for the year ending 30 June 1890. Government Printer, Melbourne, pp. 15–16.
61   Blainey G (2000) How fire shaped a continent: Australian experiences of fire since 1788. In: Fire! The Australian Experience. Proceedings of the 1999 National Academies Forum, Canberra, p. 35.
62   Lilydale Express, Friday 12 January 1962: 'Irresponsible lighting of fires'.
63   Lilydale Express, 12 January 1962.
64   Healesville Guardian, 13 May 1944.

Fire was gradually eliminated from normal daily experience as electricity took over from candles, kerosene and, eventually, even wood stoves (although it was an electrical fault that started the Kilmore East fire on Black Saturday). Firewood for the home became more recreational. 'Smoke nights' – once part of the fabric of social life and an especially masculine ritual – went into decline as smoking itself became a health issue. Instead of being a social accompaniment and enhancement, smoking was pushed to the margins of social life, even becoming anti-social. Things had changed since 1939 when the Red Cross, 'concerned about the health of the bush fire refugees' as they emerged from the smoking forests, appealed to the public for 'gifts of tobacco'.[65] Even for

Workers employed to cut timber for bushfire victims receive their tobacco rations, c. 1944.
(Argus Newspaper Collection of Photographs, State Library of Victoria)

victims of fire, smoke was then considered a balm. By the 1970s smoke was becoming an infamous irritant and outdoor smoke and 'burning off' followed suit.[66] Just when more systematic controlled burning of forests was being advocated by fire managers, public smoke was becoming less tolerated. An ecological critique of fuel-reduction burns was also gathering strength.

Dugouts

There was a period in the history of fire in the tall forests of Victoria – 1930–1960 – when there emerged a distinctive and effective cultural adaptation to the deadly firestorm of the flume. Fire refuge dugouts were a product of settler bush wisdom and were a survival response to living among these distinctive trees. Few dugouts were built in other forest regions. Forest historian Peter Evans has researched the history of dugouts in Victoria and, on 7 February 2009, he was readying to face fire himself as he prepared to defend a small museum of sawmilling history on the outskirts of Alexandra. Fortunately he did not come under direct threat, but wrote later: 'I never want to come any closer than that.' Even 25 years of studying Victorian fire history did not prepare Peter for the ferocity of that night. He walked into the blackened bush after Black Saturday and saw trees ripped out by their roots and a forest that was 'essentially bare down to the mineral earth', and he could not help but think of 1939.

The dugout – a military term drawn from the underground shelters used by soldiers in the Great War during bombardments – was first used at a sawmill settlement near Powelltown in 1932 and was built by forest workers themselves. Several employees at one of George Worlley's mills near

65   'Gifts of tobacco wanted', *Age*, 25 January 1939, p. 5.

66   Cheney P (September 2004) Canberra: bush capital or bushfire capital? *Canberra Historical Journal* no. 54, pp. 17–18.

Powelltown were aware that the Black Sunday 1926 fire had taken 14 lives (including a woman and three children) at another of Worlley's mills at Mt Beenak. Therefore in early 1932, as the summer strengthened and the bush dried ominously, they started digging a trench into the hillside at the end of each working day. About a week later, on 5 February, a deadly fire bore down upon them and the men quickly threw corrugated iron over the top of the trench, covered it with earth and scrambled inside with blankets and water. There they sheltered for about two hours while the fire destroyed everything around them. In an article headed 'A Lesson from the Fires', the *Lilydale Express* commended the workers on their foresight: 'The feeling among these men now is that a dug-out will be their first consideration for safety when employed in the heavy bush country during the risky fire season.'[67]

The five men survived, but at another sawmill near Erica that had no dugout, six people died. Therefore, following these fires, the Forests Commission strongly advised sawmillers to construct efficient dugouts and also sponsored a design by one of its engineers and surveyors, Mervyn Bill. Bill believed that 36 people had already lost their lives because of the lack of refuges at bush sawmills and pointed out that fire escapes were required by regulation in all city buildings but that no law protected the inhabitants of vulnerable sawmill settlements. But many sawmillers were reluctant to follow the Forests Commission advice. They had any number of justifications: they did not want the bother and expense, believed fire would never invade the cool, moist side of the ranges, felt there were good escape routes from their mills, trusted in the protection of a nearby creek, or considered it degrading for people to cramp themselves in a hole in the ground. But some sawmillers did provide dugouts and some workers constructed them anyway. These underground refuges generally had one narrow opening that could be shielded with a blanket kept wet from water stored inside. In 1939 the efficacy of dugouts would be truly tested.

As the firestorm swept towards a mill at Tanjil Bren, 30 workers entered a large dugout where six of them at a time took turns holding a wet blanket at the door – and they all survived. At another sawmill, large trenches that had been dug for the mill machinery were quickly converted to a makeshift dugout, and the men crawled in one by one, lay down in a line and survived. At Hill End, most residents of the isolated settlement took shelter in old mine shafts and tunnels and survived. In the sawmill settlements of the Erica district, dugouts built since 1932 saved many lives.

It took courage and desperation to climb underground 'like a wombat' and, amidst smoke, panic and deafening noise, to stay there. Even where dugouts existed in 1939, many bushworkers did not trust them. People died fleeing from sawmills equipped with dugouts. At the Ruoak No. 3 mill in the Rubicon forest, workers crammed the dugout with their furniture and fled. The four slowest died. But their furniture survived, and some of it remained there even 60 years later, 'embedded in the collapsed remains of the dugout'.[68] Fred and Victor Yelland, who had sawmills at Britannia Creek and Matlock, justified their decision not to build a dugout by indicating the availability of a brick house nearby. On Black Friday, Vera Maynard sheltered in that house and died when she was unable to escape after it caught fire.

---

67   *Lilydale Express*, 12 February 1932, p. 3.

68   Evans P (1997) Refuge from fire: sawmill dugouts in Victoria. In: *Australia's Ever-Changing Forests III*. (Ed. J Dargavel) p. 222. CRES, ANU, Canberra.

At Fitzpatrick's Mill near Matlock, 15 people died and only one survived. There was no dugout and little clearing had been done around the mill in advance. Judge Stretton wrote:

At one mill, desperate but futile efforts were made to clear of inflammable scrub the borders of the mill and mill settlement. All but one person at that mill were burned to death, many of them while trying to burrow to imagined safety in the sawdust heap. Horses were found, still harnessed in their stalls, dead, their limbs fantastically contorted. The full story of the killing of this small community is one of unpreparedness, because of apathy and ignorance and perhaps of something worse.

Perhaps of something worse … Stretton meant culpable negligence. The fires of 1919, 1926 and 1932 had delivered lessons that some were criminally determined to ignore.

Ruby Lorkin, who lived at the Ada No. 2 sawmill near Powelltown and refused to leave her husband, Harold Lorkin, who was foreman, survived the Black Friday fire in a dugout that was hastily excavated the afternoon before. In 1984, she recalled her ordeal:

I had only walked a few yards down the wooden tramline to the mill, when a torch of burning bark fell at my feet and set the line alight. My husband called 'Run, run for your life into the dug-out'. I dropped the tea billies and food and ran. The men were still frantically soaking the mill. When they saw it was no use they were forced to come into the dug-out. How we lived through that dreadful inferno I shall never know.

It was 113 degrees in Melbourne so you can imagine how awfully hot it was there as the worst fires in Australian history swept over us, sweeping sawmill, houses, horses, everything before it. I think, maybe, because it went so quickly, fanned by a terrific north wind behind it was the reason we survived. We two women were told to lie down on the ground whilst water was thrown over us, until the water reached boiling point and we could not drink it. Four men at a time stood at the small opening of the dug-out holding up soaking blankets until the blankets dried, caught alight and were swept from their hands in a few moments, then another four went forward to take their place. The Engineer went berserk and tried to take his wife outside and had to be quietened by knocking him unconscious to save his life. The next morning, when the fire had gone taking our homes and all our possessions, we crawled out although our clothes were riddled by sparks which fell down through the small funnel the men had put in for a chimney and the men's hands were badly scorched by holding up the blankets. Strangely, no one was badly burned.[69]

Although sheltering in a dugout was often deeply traumatic in the way Ruby Lorkin described, dozens of people did survive the fire by going underground. In fact if dugouts and mining tunnels had not been there to protect people in 1939, the death toll of Black Friday would have been similar to that of Black Saturday.

69   This account is quoted in Evans P, 'Refuge from fire', p. 216.

Three people did die in a dugout in 1939. Sawmiller Ben Saxton had wisely built the large dugout at his Tanjil Bren sawmill that saved the lives of 30 of his workers. He had also built a smaller dugout near his own home at the mill and this is where Saxton, his wife Dorothy, and a young timber worker, Michael Gorey, retreated as the fire approached. It was possibly social pressures that made the mill manager and his wife segregate themselves from the main body of workers. The front of the dugout apparently caught fire and collapsed, knocking down Saxton and suffocating the others. Peter Evans considers that the larger dugout was safer not only structurally but also because there were more men to hold wet blankets at the entrance, a job they had to rotate frequently because of the intense heat.[70]

Peter Evans concluded that the 1939 fires 'demonstrated without doubt the efficacy of dugouts as a refuge from fire'. Most sawmillers were eager to construct them after 1939 and the Australian Timber Workers Union instructed their members not to accept employment at any mill unless the installation of a dugout was the first work carried out at the site.

Dugouts and tunnels were also used by other bush dwellers who knew their homes weren't safe in a firestorm. In 1939, some Steels Creek residents sheltered in mining adits. At Dixons Creek, Maria Taylor recalled how her family waited anxiously as they heard news of other fires during the days before Black Friday. Her brother Jim put bikes, guns and rifles in the dry dam and dug a hole in the garden near the house where he buried one suitcase containing good clothes and valuables and another huge suitcase containing

A Terrifying Experience – *a family seeks refuge in the river at Warrandyte in 1939. (From the* Argus, *14 January 1939, National Library of Australia)*

70   Evans P, 'Refuge from fire', p. 224.

the contents of his sister Hilda's glory box. Jim and brother Fred then set to work digging a dugout in the creek bank. When it seemed certain the fires would come through their property, the boys took their mother and Hilda in the truck to the dugout, and stocked it with stools, rugs, food and a thermos or two of tea. The boys hung a wet blanket at the opening. There they stayed 'in that place of safety about four and a half hours during that fateful afternoon' as the fire passed along the bank overhead. In 1983, during the Ash Wednesday fires at McMahons Creek, 83 people survived by huddling day and night in a floodwater tunnel at the Yarra Dam.

By 2009, many of the old forest dugouts had collapsed or decayed and some had been destroyed because they were seen to be unsafe, casualties of our ever more litigious society. The original reason for them being there appeared to have been forgotten – or perhaps we felt that our society had outgrown them? However, on Black Saturday, some Steels Creek residents survived with the help of makeshift 'refuges'. Joe and Pat Maurovic used their stone cellar as an improvised fire bunker, a place of retreat from which they could occasionally rush to beat out flames. Dorothy Barber sheltered under her house in a small cavity beside a concrete water tank, where she sat on a ledge beside the powerless water pump. It was the only part of her house that survived. Her son walked in at midnight grimly expecting to find a corpse, but there was Dorothy emerging from the ground and from the ashes.

* * *

Linocuts by Ivan Filsell.

The story of *Black Saturday at Steels Creek* has been told in detail, with the help of residents of the valley, by our colleague the historian, Peter Stanley, in a separate book of that name. Many of the experiences that were strange or shocking on that day can be found embedded in this local history of fire that we have just explored: the way fire swept down from the northern ranges and could also burn destructively from the south, the confusion of winds on a single day, the ember attack from the distant tall trees, the flames leaping ahead of the fire front, the thundering roar, the exploding fireballs, the giant trees ripped out by the roots or sheered off at ground level, the fatal effects of the cool change, the desperate late evacuations, the sheltering in dams, paddocks and makeshift refuges, the heroism. Fire, like flood, tends to revisit the same places. Vegetation, topography and climate conspire to

invite it back, no matter what humans do. The point of surveying 150 years of bushfires and firestorms is to try to secure the memory of these recurrent experiences. They are written into the history of the valley – and into its future.

The 1898 fire recalled 1851; 1926 encapsulated 1919 and 1914; 1932 was 1926 all over again; 1939 was the worst ever – each was the worst ever – but 1939 was the climax of a crescendo of fires and also a reprise of 1851; 1962 equalled in ferocity the 'never-to-be-forgotten' 1939; 1983 was a horrible concentration of 1939 and 1962; and 2009 was … 'unprecedented'? Even though there were new elements to Black Saturday – the high death toll and the sense that it was a fire exacerbated by climate change – the most haunting aspect of the event was its familiarity. The same images, the same stories, the same words and

phrases, and the same frightening and awesome natural force that we find so hard to remember and perhaps unconsciously strive to forget. It is a recurrent nightmare. We know this phenomenon, we know the specific contours of the event, and we even know how people live and how people die. The climate change scenario is frightening. But even worse is the knowledge that we still have not come to terms with what we have already experienced.

Part of what is so moving about the saga of Black Saturday is the way it collapsed time, not just the time for decision as the terrible fire descended upon the valley, but also the time of a century as people found themselves again in an age-old elemental battle amongst the stringybark. Twenty-first century people with pumps and fire plans were beating out flames with bits of old carpet. There is something utterly humbling and purifying in that equalisation across time, something terrifying and transcendental all at once. And the stories generated by the trauma of 2009 were like those of yore; they were about innocence and tragedy, heroism and grim humour.

But important differences also emerge. Evacuation was normal in all those fires. For most of the history of Steels Creek, including its long Aboriginal history, no one believed their houses were safe. Auntie Nellie was extracted by force from her home and most people fled of their own accord. A 'safe place' was a creek, a bare or ploughed paddock, a safely prepared or quickly excavated dugout, a mining adit or tunnel, or just somewhere else. If you were trapped at home, there was an art to abandoning it at the right moment. The acknowledged vulnerability of homes made it essential for those caught in them to get out. And people in those earlier times were more inclined to look out the window, go outside and watch the horizon, sniff the air. In 2009, the internet was a killer. The private, domestic computer screen with its illusion of omniscience and instant communication compounded the vulnerability and isolation of the home.

Black Saturday

Steels Creek, February, March, April 2009.

Photographs: 1-10, 13 and 17 James Calder; 11, 12 Christine Hansen; 14 and 18-21 Julia Fahey; 15, 16 Sally Ferres and Dave Gormly; 22-25 Bronwyn Dahlstrom.

Home

Christine Hansen

On a property not far from the Pinnacle Lane turn-off, a row of eucalypts follows a fence line over a rise and down towards the creek, defining the perimeter of the small acreage. Further into the Steels Creek valley, past the grapevines and vegie patches, the tennis courts and the Community Centre, another track leads off to the left and up a sharp ascent to the Kinglake National Park. Between these two points the cleared valley floor is dotted with houses and sheds. If these structures can't all be seen from the road, the gates and letterboxes that crowd the verge hint at their location.

The view across this valley, with its patchwork of forests, grazing and grapes and its houses nestled into folds or perching on ridges, is satisfying to the

eye. It is a place that can be inhabited in a way that is both sustaining and sustainable: it is a place to make a home. The charred skeletons of trees that have prickled the ridgelines since the fires of February 2009, however, remind us that this is not just a place of nurture and comfort. When the creek is flowing it is difficult to remember that the complex of forces which carved this landscape converge not often but regularly in a devastating conflagration. And when the moment for it to ignite arrives, each element plays a role in the story that unfolds.

That these devastating fires happen regularly but infrequently is one of their most dangerous features. By the time another large fire is due, a generation has come and gone and nobody much remembers the one before. In the intervening years we come to believe that we know this place intimately. We examine its potential for growing and grazing through soil analysis and hydrology. We navigate its features by engineering roads around its watercourses and up its steep inclines. We walk in it, paint it, plant gardens in it; we even fight bushfires in it. And most of all we know it through living in it: choosing sites, building houses, installing drainage and sewerage systems, connecting power and erecting fences. We believe we understand this valley, this landscape, this country and in understanding it we feel safe. Yet we can't escape the blackened ridgeline that, for the moment at least, frames the verdant valley and challenges our feelings of home as a safe harbour.

If we are to understand the forces at work in this place, we need to understand the clash of ideas embedded in the landscape and the layers of history that both exacerbate and obscure the conflict they cause. We need to see this site not just as a familiar and in many ways unremarkable corner of peri-urban life, but as an archive of ideas about place and home.

* * *

The fenced house site just up from the Pinnacle Lane turn-off marks the location of the first substantial building constructed in the Steels Creek valley, built by George Fletcher sometime in the mid 19th century. It is 50 years since a house stood on the site, but the treed line reminds us that this landscape is formed as much by culture as by nature. Building fences was the first task of immigrant settlers and fenced house sites such as this were a way of domesticating the 'wild' landscape, remaking it in the image of the homes they had left.

By the time Fletcher pegged out this fence line, he may well have had a hankering for his past. He was just 21 years old when he left his friends and family in Herefordshire England, but he was 37 before the Victorian Amending Land Act of 1865 offered him the chance of a new beginning. The 16-year wait as a miner and labourer had prepared him. When the new legislation offered an opportunity to 'select' some property Fletcher jumped. Within 18 months of the Act being passed he had selected a choice 80 acres of the Steels Creek valley with a further 320 acres following not long after.

Although the Messrs Bell and Armstrong had made their mark as the first 'owners' of the valley, it was Fletcher who prepared the ground for the first 'permanent' house in 1867 in Steels Creek. He no doubt felled and shaped the timbers himself, stripped the pliable and waterproof stringybark for roofing, plugged the holes in the loosely clad walls with mud render from the building site and fashioned a chimney from whatever materials he had to hand. But his most absorbing task would have been to walk the recently surveyed boundaries of his property, seeing its potential to become the cleared fields and fenced paddocks of his dreams; a place of his own, where his livestock could grow fat and his crops could flourish under southern skies. And as he walked and built and dreamed, he unwittingly sowed the land with indelible traces of his past.

Four hundred acres was a property of unimaginable riches for a poor Herefordshire lad such as Fletcher. Where he came from, the average farm size in the mid 1800s was 78 acres. He had grown up in a landscape made of these smallholdings, each growing oats and wheat, perhaps an apple or pear orchard, some small-scale vegetable crops, with larger farms extending to herds of cattle as well as sheep for wool and meat. The patchwork of fields and fences that flowed over the misty hills on the border of England and Wales had shaped his view of the world. These vistas of open farmland had been formed before memory began; the gentle slopes were already mostly treeless from the time of the Bronze Age, nearly 4000 years before. For 2000 years, the stone fences added by the Celts had enclosed fields for crops and pasture. The Romans arrived to plant straight lines of grapes and breed the hardy cattle that would become famous around the globe. The Anglo-Saxons moved in and developed the three-field system, which became the basis of

medieval agriculture. In the late Middle Ages villagers started to rationalise the field strips by purchase or exchange. Under Acts of Parliament beginning in 1607, not just fenced fields but large previously public tracts of land began to move into private hands, the exclusive property of a single owner. The drive towards private ownership grew over the ensuing 200 years and by the time young George Fletcher emerged on the scene, the divide between rich and poor, landed gentry and bonded labour, city and country cast a shadow over the population.[1]

All of this fencing and farming, acquiring and trading, carved the Herefordshire countryside into its distinctive shape. Property and law, families and food were bound together in the landscape, the vistas telling the story of long human occupation. When crops failed and famine hit in the mid 19th century many of the youngest and fittest left to find a new life elsewhere, taking with them not much more than their deeply rooted history and their hopes for the future. George Fletcher was one of them.

If Fletcher unwittingly sowed the history of his homeland into the Steels Creek valley as he fenced his pasture and bred his cattle, he wasn't the only one to do so. Nor was he the first. Ten years before his construction work began, another Englishman had walked the same tracks and trails in the service of a much more radical, although invisible, intervention. The impressively bewhiskered but painfully arthritic District Surveyor, Clement Hodgkinson, led a party of workers on the 60 km trek from Melbourne to carry out the first survey of the area in 1856.[2] With their arcane equipment of theodolites, chains,

1   Herefordshire Council (2011) *Historic Environment*. Education series.

2   Nunn HW (1972) Hodgkinson, Clement (1818–1893). *Australian Dictionary of Biography*. National Centre of Biography, Australian National University, http://adb.anu.edu.au/biography/hodgkinson-clement-3774/text5959, accessed 26 April 2011.

slide rules and dumpy poles, this little group planted an entirely new language into the landscape. What had been a cohesive geography of interconnected Wurundjeri country began its transformation into sequestered private property as it was overwritten by words such as county, parish, acre and rood. These words, grounded in the long history of another place, took over as the primary descriptors of the billabongs, creeks, ridges and forests that formed the valley and its surrounds. As the words were hammered into the rock along with the trig points, the landscape was captured on paper as an *idea*, one that could be carried back to Melbourne and viewed from the comfort of Spring Street. Once the first map of the area was lodged in the Surveyor General's Office, decisions about the future development of this place could, for the first time, be made from a remote location.

The English-born, French-trained Hodgkinson was an astute observer and a talented engineer. On returning to Melbourne he made a number of predictions about the area (see opposite).

How right he was: as any Steels Creek local can tell you, winter is a time of bogged tractors and muddy boots. And as any epicurean can tell you, the Upper Yarra Valley is indeed some of the best grape growing country in Australia, if not the world.

Not surprisingly, Hodgkinson went on to become the assistant commissioner and secretary of the new Board of Crown Lands and Survey and helped to draft the Lands Act of which George Fletcher would one day take advantage. As his map of Burgoyne and Tarrawarra attests, he was a talented practitioner of a craft which was steeped in the logic and lore of land measuring dating back to antiquity and beyond: recent evidence suggests that even the makers of Stonehenge used surveying techniques of peg and rope geometry. This highly sophisticated field held within it the histories of mathematics, land tenure laws and precision instrument manufacture. When Hodgkinson and his helpers dragged their linen tape measures and metal chains through the boggy marshes of the Upper Yarra Valley, they laid a web of logarithmic and trigonometric calculations over the surface. The ground for an agricultural future, as he saw it, had been laid. For all his ability to conjure imaginary dairy farms, vineyards and roads from within the language of measuring, however, Hodgkinson was unable to read other more ancient languages written into the landscape. This blindness led to a crucial omission. Although he noticed the stringybarks and box eucalypts, he couldn't see their deep biological past, nor their inevitable future. From the list of qualities so prominently featured on his beautifully drafted map, one fundamental element is missing: fire.

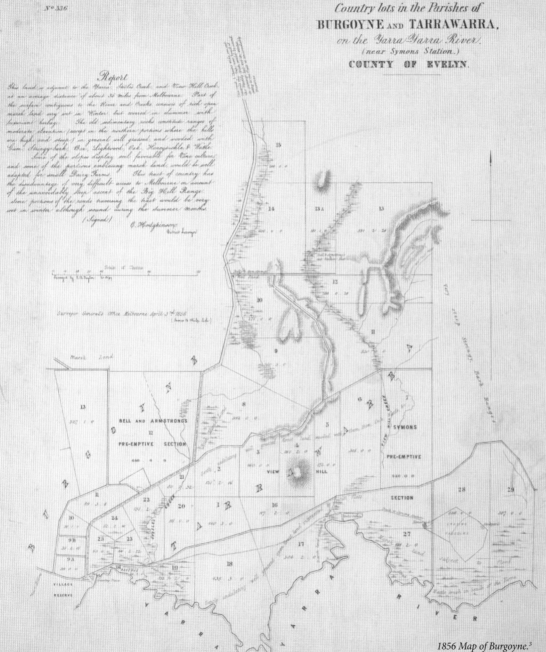

1856 Map of Burgoyne.[3]

County lots in the Parishes of Burgoyne and Tarrawarra, County of Evelyn

This land is adjacent to the Yarra, Steele's Creek, and View Hill Creek, at an average distance of about 35 miles from Melbourne. Part of the surface contiguous for the River and Creeks, consists of rich open marsh land very wet in Winter, but covered in Summer with luxuriant herbage. The old sedimentary rocks constitute ranges of moderate elevation (except in the northern portions where the hills are high and steep) in general well grassed, and wooded with Gum, Stringybark, Box, Lightwood, Oak, Honeysuckle, & Wattle.

Some of the slopes display soil favourable for Vine culture, and some of the portions embracing marsh land would be well adapted for small Dairy Farms. This tract of country has the disadvantage of very difficult access to Melbourne on account of the unavoidably steep ascent of the Big Hill Range. Some portions of the roads traversing the tract would be very wet in winter although sound during the Summer months.

C. Hodgkinson 1856

3   State Library of Victoria, MAPS 820 BJE
1837- BURGOYNE 1856 Country lands in the parishes of Burgoyne and Tarrawarra on the Yara Yarra River (near Symons station) County of Evelyn.

To be fair to Hodgkinson, western intellectual traditions of his time were limited in their capacity to describe the foreign and complex fire-dependent bio-systems he was mapping. It took until the late 20th century before international fire historian Stephen Pyne found a term that expressed the intricate interplay between the geography, weather patterns and plant biology of this place. He called it the 'fire flume'.[4]

Despite having experienced the 'Black Thursday' fires of 1851 in which nearly 5 million hectares of Victoria were burnt, including the area they were mapping, fire was still far from the minds of the early survey teams.[5] Their priority, having measured the land, was to name it. Surnames of settlers, nostalgic allusions to homelands, literary references and statements of political authority such as the names of colonial administrators, aristocrats or English royalty were all popular choices. Maps started to fill as the 'empty' landscape took form: Victoria and Melbourne, Port Phillip, Christmas Hills, Kinglake, St Andrews and Steels Creek. With so many names to find in such a short time, other words were also called on to fill the voids: Tarrawarra, Yarra, Yering, Warrandyte, Wonga, Toolangi. These words from the Woiwurrung language of the

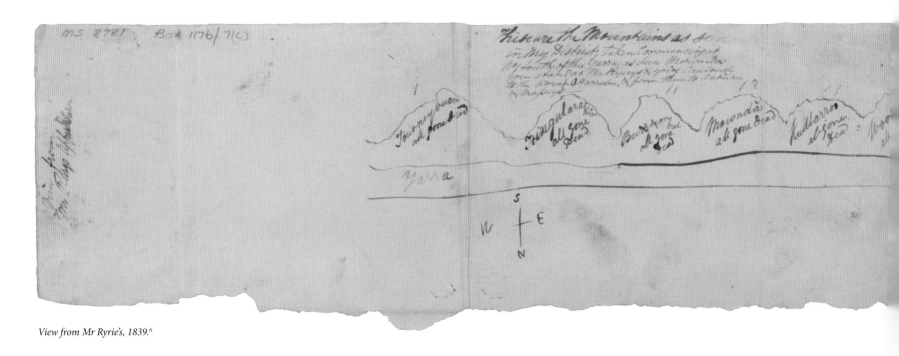

View from Mr Ryrie's, 1839.[6]

4   For a full description of the flume, see this volume, Chapter 2 'Bush' by Tom Griffiths.

5   Clode D (2010) *A Future in Flames*. Melbourne University Publishing, Melbourne.

6   State Library of Victoria MS8781, box 76/7 (c) La Trobe Library collection.

Wurundjeri people gave a distinctive flavour to the region, with their claim to 'localness'. Their actual meaning, however, was of less interest to the map makers: translations were rarely appended to the official records.

In calling on these words to fill their maps, the surveyors were following a venerable tradition. Many Aboriginal tribes were known for their naming practices and the Yarra Valley locals were no exception. As one early linguist wrote 'Not a point or inlet, knoll or dell, glade or thicket, rock or rivulet, but was designated in the language, and faithfully delineated in the memory of the ancient inhabitants.'[7] What Hodgkinson and his fellow cartographers failed to understand was that Woiwurrung names were not just linguistic decoration but held in place a knowledge system not entirely different from their own. By the time the first maps were drawn, the Wurundjeri had been measuring their country for millennia. It was divided not into parishes and properties delineated by cadastral boundaries and fences but into camping places, ceremony places, women's places, men's places, meeting places, hunting places, initiation places, birthing places. It was measured with bare feet in footsteps and named in a language given to them by the original ancestor

7   McKenzie A (1874) Specimens of native Australian languages. Cited by Wesson S (1994) *An Overview of the Sources for a Language and Clan Atlas of Eastern Victoria and Southern New South Wales*. Graduate School of Environmental Science, Monash University, Melbourne, p. 15.

beings, the creators of this country. The names held complex information on geography, seasons, resources and travel routes as well as cultural information about who could and could not use various sites. This mapping was not recorded on paper but in song and ceremony, passed in oral tradition from one generation to the next.

Occasionally, however, some local knowledge did make it onto paper and into the archives. The sketch of the 'View from Mr Ryrie's' that depicts the hills surrounding the property at Yering drawn in 1839, for example, opens a crack wide enough for us to see through to a fragment of the Wurundjeri world.[8] What is revealed hints at both the devastating loss they experienced and the ensuing loss of local knowledge that has haunted our understanding of this place ever since. The annotations on the sketch were apparently dictated by 'an old wandering black, *Kurburra*' to the 'Assistant Protector and Guardian of Aboriginals' William Thomas. To all but three of the 14 hills depicted, the words 'all gone dead' have been added. This sad rollcall of absent countrymen is accompanied by the names of the hills, including those that surround the Steels Creek valley: *Wyenondable*, *Wyeringbeik*, *Kook Kirra*, *Tarawarra*. If Kurburra offered a translation of this lexicon of landscape, Thomas did not record it. But contemporary local historian Mick Woiwood has pieced together fragments from language lists to decipher the meaning of the names. He tells us that '*Wyen* or *Wien* in the Woiwurrung language of the Wurundjeri translates as 'fire'; *Wyenondable* may therefore translate as 'the hills of fire' or the 'place of fires'.[9]

These Hills of Fire are known today as Christmas Hills. They owe their name to an emancipated convict and shepherd, David Christmas, who, having wandered lost for many days in the dense bush, emerged onto the rocky ridges from where he made his way home. The association with Mr Christmas and his happy ending is certainly a piece of interesting local history and connects the contemporary community with the settler past. But if the translation offered by Woiwood is correct, the name 'Christmas Hills' paints a further layer of culture over a deeper biological history and ongoing reality. If Surveyor Hodgkinson had known the meaning of the local naming words, he might have incorporated the knowledge into his map. The psychological difference between living in the *County of Fiery Hills* instead of the *County of Evelyn* is one we might consider, given the nature of this country.

Regardless of their contemporary name, the Hills of Fire still sit within a complex Woiwurrung cosmology, including a calendar that predicts when they will be at their most dangerous. Each season of the calendar 'is marked by the movement of the stars in the night sky and changes in the weather, coinciding with the life cycles of plants and animals'.[10] There are not four seasons but seven. Some years a season may fail to arrive but seasons either side will be extended and intense. The transition from one season to another is a dance of shifting cycles as the year revolves through the stages of birth, death and rebirth.

8   Fels M (1989) The La Trobe Library Collection of the Papers of Assistant Protector W. Thomas. *La Trobe Literary Journal* **11** (43, Autumn), 15.

9   Woiwood M and Andrew Ross Museum (2010) *The Christmas Hills Story: Once Around the Sugarloaf II*. Andrew Ross Museum, pp. 41–42.

10   All information on the Kulin Calendar comes from Museum Victoria 'Tall Forests' exhibition. Also see Allen L 'Coranderrk Calendar' (2001). In *Forests of Ash: An Environmental History*. (Ed. T Griffiths) , Cambridge University Press, Melbourne, pp. 58–59.

Waring *Wombat Season [April–July]*

Cool, rainy days follow misty mornings. A time of high rainfall and low temperatures. Waring (wombats) emerge to bask and graze in the sunshine. Bulen-bulen (superb lyrebird) males perform their courtship displays. Hearts of kombadik *(soft tree ferns) are the major food when no fruits are available. Days are short and nights are long. The constellation of Sagittarius rises in the south-east after sunset, indicating the mid point of cold weather.*

Guling *Orchid Season [August]*

Cold weather is coming to an end. Guling (orchids) are flowering. Ae-noke (caterpillars) of common brown butterfly feed on grasses at night. Muyan (silver wattles) are flowering. Bulen-bulen (superb lyrebird) males perform the last of their courtship displays. The star Arcturus is seen on the north-western horizon soon after sunset. Gurrborra (koalas) begin mating. Males bellow at night. Temperatures are rising but the rain continues. Flax-lilies are flowering.

Poorneet *Tadpole Season [September–October]*

Temperatures are rising but the rain continues. Flax-lilies are flowering. Pied currawongs call loudly and often. The flowering of plants such as myrnong (yam daisy) indicates the tubers are ready for eating. Bulen-bulen (superb lyrebird) males have finished displaying. Days and nights are of equal length.

Buath Gurru *Grass Flowering Season [November]*

The weather is warm, and it is often raining. Kangaroo grass is flowering. Buliyong (bats) are catching insects in flight. Balayang, the Creation Being, is also referred to as the bat. Male common brown butterflies are flying. Coranderrk (Victorian Christmas bush) is coming into flower. The Orion constellation is setting in the western sky around sunrise.

Kangaroo-apple Season *[December]*

Changeable, thundery weather. Dhuling (Goannas) are active. Buliyong (bats) are catching insects in flight. Days are long and nights are short. Fruits appear on kangaroo-apple bushes. Bali (cherry ballart) is fruiting. Bundjil (wedge-tailed eagles) are breeding. Bundjil, the Creation Being, is also referred to as the 'eaglehawk'.

Biderap *Dry Season [January–February]*

Hot, dry weather. High temperatures and low rainfall. Female common brown butterflies are flying. Bowat (tussock-grass) is long and dry. The Southern Cross is high in the south at sunrise.

Iuk *Eel Season [March]*

Hot winds cease and temperatures cool. Iuk (eels) are fat and ready to harvest. Binap (manna gum) is flowering. Days and nights are of equal length. Lo-An Tuka, the Hunter, is the star Canopus, seen almost due south at sunset.

Courtesy of Museum Victoria (see p. 8, footnote 10)

As well as the seven regular seasons there are two other non-annual seasons. One of these is a season of water and the other a season of fire. A big water season is likely to occur about every 25 years and a big fire season is likely to occur about every seven years. Every now and then big water and big fire will be beyond their average intensity. They will be catastrophic. But they will never arrive without warning.

The Woiwurrung had been observing this interconnected cycle of six or seven seasons, sometimes eight or even nine, played out by the plants, animals and stars over millennia. This was a calendar specific to this place, to these hills and valleys, rivers and creeks, forests and grasslands. For all its ability to integrate subtle local knowledge, however, the calendar was never adopted by the new settlers. Given their resistance to learning about the Wurundjeri, it is highly unlikely they were even exposed to it. To them these southern hemisphere weather patterns, governed (we now know) by El Niño/La Niña events in the Pacific Ocean, were mysterious and unpredictable. The years of big water and big fire were seen to sit outside the cycles of change. They were disasters, not seasons. European understanding of seasons had been carved by the northern hemisphere year, regulated by the Gulf Stream that flowed in with the Atlantic Ocean. The words that described the clearly defined quarters of the year – spring, summer, autumn, winter – were rooted too deeply, tied too tightly to language and culture to be cast aside by the new settlers. The shifting Wurundjeri cycles that could help the newcomers understand when conditions were building to a year of big water or big fire were replaced by the static European quartered year: spring, summer, autumn, winter. Another stratum was laid over the landscape and the danger further obscured.

* * *

Whatever cultural orthodoxies they bought with them, and whatever their resistance to local knowledge, the first settlers in the valley were extremely skilled. They were also observant and, within their frames of reference, highly adaptive. One thing they knew was how to build a house. No flimsy temporary campsites, these original homes were made to last. George Fletcher's house stood for over 100 years. Gulf Station, the house of his neighbour, William Bell, is still standing. Today it is owned by the National Trust, revered in heritage circles as one of the last remaining examples of an original timber farm complex, including homestead and outbuildings, dating from the 1850s. These old 'handmade' farmhouses were hewn from local timber (a clue to their longevity perhaps) and were fitted together with wonderful precision. Nails were hard to come by in the 19th century and with such good wood to hand, it was cheaper and easier to use slab and beam joinery. Modest, durable and beautifully tailored to the landscape, the old buildings became a focus of historical awareness in the district. George's house even received its own obituary when it succumbed to its inevitable fate in 1963. On 22 February of that year, the *Healesville News* reported:

A piece of the district's history perished without a single witness on Monday night when 'The Fletchers' at Steels Creek was burned down. The house was

*one of the real pioneer homes, and believed to be the first house built at
Steels Creek. It was showing its age, true enough, but, like several others has
a historical value that cannot be compensated. The cause of the demise is a
mystery. It was ok at 11 on Monday night, but on Tuesday was just a heap
of charred rubble.*

While the silvered timbers of Fletcher's place stood firm, the generations of
shacks, cottages, farmhouses and guesthouses that sprouted up and down
the valley in his wake have mostly been wiped away by fire, both bushfire and
house fires. The history buffs of the district lament the loss of the old places
as the stories and memories they held fade further into the distance. What
we forget sometimes is that not all of them were designed to last. Unlike
the farmers such as Fletcher and Bell who intended to stay, fortune-seeking
gold-prospectors, seasonal timber workers and itinerant farmhands had
no interest in building more than rudimentary accommodation. Although
their constructions were often quirky and full of character, not to mention
ingeniously fitted with interior comforts such as fireplaces, bedrooms and
washing areas, if ever they were in the path of fire no-one would try to save
them. They were intentionally ephemeral and as such, perfectly suited to the
environment.

If the temporary residences tended towards the improvised, then the houses
of subsistence farmers that dotted the valley weren't far behind. The century
that followed Fletcher's pioneering building project was a century of new

Riddells' bagged hut, late 1920s. (Courtesy of Yarra Glen & District Historical Society)

technologies that opened up a world of do-it-yourself options. Hand adzed
slabs gave way to machine-sawn slats, while the invention of wire nails and
corrugated iron transformed the rooftops of Australia. The nation that could
turn its hand to just about anything, began a love affair with its local timber
yards and hardware stores which is still going today. The majority of the
modest homes that burgeoned in Steels Creek in the late 19th and early 20th
centuries were built by workers in the timber industry – sawmill operators
and timber cutters – or by subsistence farmers (and quite often they were
both). Their designs followed the classic lines of the worker's cottage: single or
double gabled roofs, lean-to kitchens, outhouses and verandas.

Ted Lancaster was already in his seventies when his two Clydesdales pulled his covered wagon along Steels Creek Road for the first time. It was the early 1950s and times were still tough after the war. Mr Lancaster (as he was universally known) had arrived as the new caretaker for one of the absent landowners along Hargreaves Lane, but when that fell apart, he set up camp on the property of neighbours Ivy and Arthur Arney and began a building project that would last a decade.

Ted's first digs were made from an old charcoal burner's tank. He used the 2 × 3 m steel boiler as the kitchen and living room and his wagon as the bedroom. When the wagon was no longer weatherproof and the tank sizzled through a run of hot summers, it was time to redesign. Arthur sourced three large timber packing cases that had been used for transporting Austin A30 cars from England for Ted to use as building material. They were freighted to Yarra Glen on the old steam powered goods train and from there the greengrocer's cart carried them up the valley.

Ted's new packing case hut was a modest but slightly more comfortable 3 × 4 metres, with windows for ventilation. It sported a black steel fireplace at one end – found through the classifieds of the Weekly Times – and had a roof made from timber covered in bitumen paper. But the hut was just the start. Ivy recalled that 'Gordon Hubbard who had a large sawmill in Yarra Glen generously supplied many elderly pensioners with off-cuts, saving them the trouble of gathering their own firewood.' Over the next years, Ted put these off-cuts to good use building sheds and outhouses, fences, tables and chairs, a bed, shelves, food cupboards, a mantelpiece above the fireplace, a verandah and, most importantly, kennels for his much-loved dogs. He used scraps of leather to make hinges for gates and doors, old hessian bags for upholstery and bush saplings for canes in the garden. The whole complex was a demonstration of innovation and adaptation.

When he became too old for his hut, Ted moved to live with relatives but the building remained much loved by the local community. For many years it was used by the scouts and guides as a meeting place and by local families for picnics. Everyone knew it as 'Ted's hut'.

The old hut burnt down in the 2009 fires, the last material link to one of the great characters of Steels Creek.

Ted's Hut circa 2009.

While these shacks and cottages were popping up throughout the valley, the social tracks that linked them were becoming embedded in the landscape. Over time, paths that followed surveyed boundaries became formalised as lanes and roads, often named for the family whose fence lines they circumnavigated: Hunts Lane, Adams Lane, Hargreaves Road, Harvey Road, Brennan Avenue. Similarly, properties were universally known by the name of their owners: when a property changed hands, the new occupant would refer to the name of their predecessor as a descriptor, sometimes for years afterwards. Even today, the old names stick as markers of local knowledge and historical connection.

Threaded through this accumulating settler history was an ongoing relationship with fire. Until the valley was wired into the electricity grid in the 1950s, fire powered Steels Creek domestic and public life. Stoves for cooking, fireplaces for heating and of course the hugely popular bonfire for community events, all lit and warmed and nourished the lives of the valley dwellers. No backyard was without an incinerator and no picnic was complete without a boiling billy. With this daily use of fire came a confidence in using it as a tool and many of the locals developed an instinct for the role it played in regenerating the bush. Barbara Harris remembers from her childhood in the 1930s that '[My grandmother Barbara Rolfe] was renowned for walking around with a box of matches in her pocket and she'd light fires pretty often so that her cows would get fresh growth to eat.'[11] Barbara's grandmother was not alone. It was a common practice of the mountain cattlemen to set the bush alight behind them as they drove their stock to the lowlands in autumn. This was a trick probably learnt from Aboriginal people, whose farming practices famously utilised fire to create open forests and game-attracting grasslands.

For all this confidence, however, there was also awe and respect for the forces that large fires generated. People understood that their modest weatherboard cottages were never going to provide cover in a fierce bushfire. You either got out of the valley entirely, or you had somewhere to retreat to when events turned nasty. The most important thing was to save lives and to that end

Steels Creek timber worker's cottage, late 1900s.

Steels Creek 1927.

11   Barbara Harris in community workshop, Yarra Glen, 18 November 2010.

Steels Creek Property boundaries of 1892.[12]

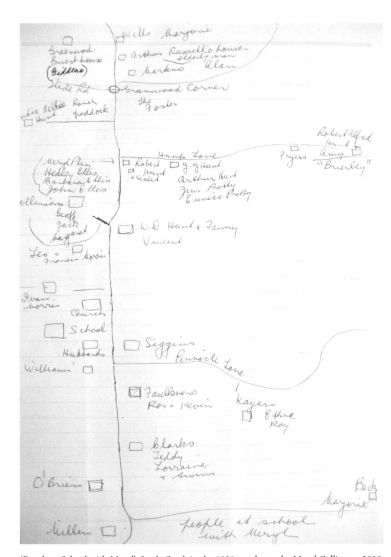

'People at School with Meryl'. Steels Creek in the 1930s as drawn by Meryl Collinson, 2010.

12   State Library of Victoria, MAP RM 2741/245 1892Victoria. Dept. of Crown Lands and Survey. Burgoyne, County of Evelyn.

there was another architectural development – the bunker. The bunker was an innovation instituted by forestry workers, who knew a thing or two about bushfires. On arriving at a new logging site they would dig a large trench into the side of a creek bank or gully, cover the trench with logs and backfill with a thick cover of soil. This shady retreat provided a respite from the heat in summer as a 'smoko' room, and offered a last resort refuge in the case of bushfire.[13] It is rumoured that there is a bunker dug into the bank behind the old schoolhouse (now the Community Centre). With the safety of the local children an understandable priority, it would be a logical addition to the community's assets.

* * *

In the last half of the 20th century, having struggled through two World Wars and a Depression, Steels Creek changed gear with a major demographic shift. As the suburbs of Melbourne spread and the aspirations of many turned to living on small acreage properties, the valley became a popular destination. The newcomers weren't only full-time residents: social groups built clubhouses, families built weekenders and animal lovers built stables and kennels. For the first time in its long history of human occupation, the valley was increasingly becoming home to people who were not economically dependent on local resources. Not surprisingly, the type of homes being built reflected this shift. At the same time as the valley demographics were reshaping, a new building technology became dominant.

27 May 1939. Dorothy Walker at the remains of the Parkinson house, 306 Steels Creek Road. (Courtesy of Yarra Glen & District Historical Society)

When a Geelong entrepreneur first tested brick veneer as a building technique in 1903, many were sceptical. Constructed around a flimsy wooden frame which held up the roof, panelling on the inside walls and a skin of bricks on the outside, the new construction method was too innovative to be embraced without suspicion. By the 1930s, however, the method was considered reliable enough for banks to approve building loans and by the 1950s, spurred by a post-war shortage of building materials, brick veneer had almost entirely replaced double brick construction in Victoria. The success of the 'project home' in Australia had begun and it would change the face of Australia's urban and rural environments forever. Steels Creek was no

13   Barry Smith in conversation with author at Yarra Glen and District Historical Society, 2 March 2010.

exception and the vista of pasture and bush land became increasingly dotted with brick veneer homes as the century wore on. The valley still boasted many timber dwellings: some of them were historic while others were built as new constructions (including those conceived as a conscious aesthetic departure from the dominance of brick veneer). The modest 'kit' house, both timber and fibreboard, was also well represented, standing in for the old 'ephemeral' cottages.

Whether timber or brick, old or new, all of these constructions sat within a complex cultural and historical context that was so deeply familiar it remained largely unobserved. Over the course of one and a half centuries, structures and systems that had their roots in the deep past of other places increasingly shaped the landscape: roads, lanes, fences and boundaries carved the valley into a patchwork of discrete parcels of land as the contemporary vista we call 'Steels Creek' began to emerge. Within these formations, the social geography of the valley flourished and layers of social history accumulated. The valley dwellers 'belonged' to these patterns of tracks and trails. Deep connections were formed as people built their houses, raised their families, gardened the soil, walked the pathways, painted the vistas, photographed the wildlife, celebrated the seasons, and performed all the other myriad actions of creating a 'home'.

Before the events of 7 February 2009, the last major fire to enter the valley was in 1962, before that 1939. Several others had threatened and one or two had nibbled at the edges (doing some peripheral damage in Steels Creek and much damage in neighbouring communities), but the 'big one' had skipped over them. As time passed, connection to hands-on knowledge of fire grew distant: the '1939' and '1962' generations who might have offered living testimony became fewer, fire was no longer central to public and private life and the new arrivals in the valley had little, if any, inherited family knowledge of this place and its fire history. Coupled with this loss of local knowledge was the fact that most of the houses built in the last half of the 20th century, particularly the brick veneer buildings which offered a contrary appearance, were manifestly inadequate to provide proper refuge in a serious fire.

The valley dwellers were not unaware of the risk or unprepared for fire. Many community members had attended Fireguard training offered by the local fire authorities. Many had installed extensive fire fighting equipment around their homes. Many had participated in community 'fire ready' events, including taking roles in 'phone trees' and other communication strategies. Many had even fought fires in volunteer brigades. Yet on the day the inevitable fire arrived, a disaster of catastrophic proportions unfolded leaving locals gasping 'we had no idea what we were preparing for'. The statistics alone tell the story: Of the estimated **95 houses which were standing** in the Steels Creek locality on 7 February 2009, **67 of them were burnt to the ground**.[14] Within five of those buildings, 10 people lost their lives.

The loss that these numbers contain confirms a truth so brutal it is almost unspeakable: fire doesn't care about counties and parishes, names and maps, fence lines and house sites, lived history, social geography or even life. When

14   These figures are compiled from local records with the assistance of Linda Leckie, Building Services, Yarra Ranges Council (as at February 2011).

the landscape is stripped bare of its human story all that remains are the elements which conduct flames: the folds of the earth which channel winds, the biology of the forests which determine flammability and the patterns of weather which govern heat and moisture. The flume.

The current generation of Steels Creek residents are now the lineage holders of a truth about their home that no amount of accumulated social history can ever overwrite: the essential biological imperative of this place is *to burn*.

The fires will not happen often but when they do, the resulting firestorm will likely be of an unsurvivable magnitude. The task they are left with is how to leave that story embedded in the landscape after the bush has grown back and the people have moved on. As new buildings spring up in place of the burnt houses, many are reflecting on the stories that have formed their design decisions. The following four houses tell the story of fire and people in very different ways. Together they show the emergence of a truly adaptive architecture that might hold the message of the 2009 firestorm into the future.

Four houses

Margaret and John Houston

The elegant home of Margaret and John Houston sits high on the slopes of the Yarra Ridge escarpment. The large glass doors across the front offer a magnificent view along the length of the Steels Creek valley and the deep horizon beyond. These days the view is a little wider than they're used to. 'We had to put in blinds since the fire. We couldn't have breakfast in comfort,' Margaret explains. With the bush gone, at least for the moment, the contours of the crests and dips are exposed in a way they've not seen before. The Kinglake plateau rises behind them and the Yarra Valley, into which Steels Creek flows, diminishes into a blue haze to the south.

Margaret and John were at home on Saturday 7 February 2009, when the firestorm rushed at them from several directions. It was terrifying, but they were prepared: they had been prepared for more than 20 years. Bushfire had been their first concern when they designed the house in 1983 but until 2009 their planning had never been tested. Like many people in the valley, the Houstons were originally from the city. Although they loved their home in Melbourne, they also loved to garden and in 1982 they decided to expand their horizons, in every sense, with a move to Steels Creek. It was one of the few places, not too far from friends and family, offering what they were looking for. Before development restrictions were introduced towards the end of the 1980s, several of the old farms were divided into lots as small as 10 acres and sold as 'lifestyle' blocks – perfect for their needs. Margaret and John fell in love with both the views and the chance to realise their dream of an expansive native garden. In 1982 they set up a caravan on their new land and began to think about what to build. Before they could finalise a design, one of the great disasters of 20th century Australia hit the ranges surrounding Melbourne: the Ash Wednesday bushfires.

View from the front patio.

On 16 February 1983 a band of cold air hovering in the Great Australian Bight pulled blistering desert winds from central Australia towards the south. After 10 months of severe drought, the hot winds hit the heavily timbered and tinder dry hills of South Australia and Victoria in ferocious gusts. South-east Australia was sweltering and the 'flume' was in full force. It took nothing more than a branch against a power line for a fire to start. Once alight, there was little that could be done to stop it. Before the rains that came in with the cool change doused the flames, 75 people across South Australia and Victoria had been killed; in Victoria alone more than 2000 houses were burnt to the ground. It was a moment of sobering reality. A fire of this magnitude had not been seen since Black Friday of 1939. In the intervening 44 years people had forgotten the biological loyalty of the forests: they are programmed to burn.

Driving through the fire-ravaged Dandenong ranges as they travelled to and from their new block of land in 1983, Margaret and John were deeply shaken by the destruction they saw. More importantly, they were shocked at the choices people were making as they returned to the sites of devastation. Margaret was particularly surprised at how the small hamlet of Cockatoo was responding to the loss of six people from their community. She saw that 'they were rebuilding what they'd lost – timber houses in amongst all that bush. Almost exact replicas!' Aware that they too were building on a bush block, they determined to learn a lesson from the loss.

In the wake of the 1983 fires, the Country Fire Authority developed a set of guidelines for building in bushfire zones. They released a public education kit as audiocassettes with accompanying booklets to explain their recommendations and to encourage people to think about what and where they were building. The Houstons ordered a set and studied them diligently. The information completely changed their ideas about design. 'The CFA were saying you shouldn't build on a hill. We were on a foothill with a big northern face very close to the southern border of the Kinglake National Park. The last thing you should do is build in timber,' John explained. They immediately cast aside their original plans and drew up new ones incorporating all the recommendations made by the CFA.

The building site, circa 1984. (From the collection of John and Margaret Houston)

Their first revision was to use a poured concrete slab for the foundation, rather than brick and timber with an underfloor cavity. They also decided on double brick walls with cathedral ceilings as a feature. 'The ceiling follows the roofline so there is no cavity for fire to get into. There's no combustible space like there is in most houses,' John explains. The flush metal door and window frames are completely sealed to prevent spot fires from ember attacks and the open plan design allows for easy access if a fire ever did penetrate the outer walls. As well as these passive design features, they also installed extensive firefighting systems. 'We had 20 000 gallons of water in the house tank and it kept overflowing, so we thought let's put in another tank of 20 000 gallons and that can be our fire fighting tank. We put in a sprinkler system right around the house and had tank-to-tank plumbing. It led to a water reticulation system around the house then a ridge line system, with sprinklers on the roof as well as above ground sprinklers.' With their own house attended to, they began to build links to a wider network.

As in many small rural and semirural communities, fires were the topic not just of informal conversation but also of organised community events. The

Double brick interior with cathedral ceilings.

Door and window frames sit flush with the brickwork.

neighbours local to John and Margaret held an annual 'fire ready' street party, a fun opportunity to compare strategies, set up communication systems and share knowledge and resources: some people bought scanners for listening to the CFA frequencies; others drew up phone trees to ensure everyone was in the communications loop; if sprinkler systems were installed, instructions on how to work them were shared with neighbours. Not everybody had invested in precautions and not everybody was interested in participating in events – many still believed that the 'big one' would never come – but there were enough people for a collective effort to be worthwhile. For John and Margaret, everything they could do was done and one day their efforts would be tested: Saturday 7 February 2009 would be that day.

As it did for many, the speed of the fire on Black Saturday took John and Margaret by surprise. Once the fire was upon them, they realised they were in their house for the duration; the steep road down to the valley floor would have been a nightmare to navigate in the smoke and there was no guarantee that the main road to Yarra Glen would be open. Only two possibilities remained: their systems would work, or they would fail. The second possibility had unimaginable consequences.

Almost immediately the house filled with smoke. Fire alarms went off. Intense radiant heat cracked windows. The wooden pergola over the back patio caught fire. Things were not going well, but worse was yet to come. A petrol pump operated the sprinkler system that was threaded across the house. As the fire whipped embers into the air, a small spark landed on the pump and burned a hole into the plastic fuel tank. The petrol drained and the engine stopped. The sprinklers, which had been so carefully installed, were instantly rendered useless. The water tank itself was concrete and holding up well against the flames. The plumbing fittings, however, were PVC. They melted almost instantly. John and Margaret watched through their big glass windows, with smoke choking their lungs and alarms screeching in their ears, as 20 000 gallons of water, so carefully stockpiled through many long years of drought, rushed uselessly down the hill. And then the flames inched closer. The timber verandah post caught alight and began to wick fire up into the rafters. With no pump and now no water, they scrabbled to find a way to extinguish it. Margaret had a small plastic spray bottle for watering her indoor plants stashed under the kitchen sink. John grabbed it and began

Burnt veranda post which almost set the house on fire. (From the collection of John and Margaret Houston)

squirting furiously at the verandah post. The flames sizzled and died. The windows, although cracked, did not collapse. The fire front passed. The noise decreased. The smoke cleared. They had survived. Some time later they would discover that not all of their neighbours had.

In the days and months that followed the fires, the people of the valley began the impossible task of understanding what had happened. 'What ifs' and 'If onlys' were repeated over and over as the stories came into focus. Tales of courage turned to admissions of terror. The truth of what 'almost was' began to dawn on survivors: luck decided how a property was affected or whether an escape was successful. The velocity of the fire front, the timing of the wind change and the course of the ember shower combined with the subtle nuances of geography in an unending set of variables. At the Houstons', luck collided with good design. The memory of another fire is held in the architecture of their house and on the day it drew a cloak around them, even when their systems failed. Embers found no foothold in the building and the fire front passed leaving the outer walls and roof unpenetrated. Unlike others in the district, they were not hit by the unsurvivable firestorm – which didn't just burn but desiccated all in its path. There is no domestic construction that can withstand forces of that magnitude. What they did experience, however, was an extremely fierce and dangerous bushfire, one that could have proved fatal, but for their attention to planning.

Melted plumbing fittings on concrete tank. (From the collection of John and Margaret Houston)

Pump with melted fuel tank. (From the collection of John and Margaret Houston)

Margaret and John were deeply distressed by the fires. The experience of being in the house during the event, the grief at the loss within their community, and the demanding process of making insurance claims all contributed. Just how affected they were became clear as they began the job of repairing their home. John admitted 'There's an element of trauma when you're doing all this that stops you supervising things as much as you should. It was chaos. You'd just get one thing finished and another tradesman would turn up.' He was as surprised as anybody when he realised that the verandah posts and plumbing fittings had been replaced with like-for-like: wood with wood, PVC with PVC, despite both elements being the weakest points in their system. The insurance company had insisted and the Houstons were too deeply in shock to resist. Their replacement is on the to-do list.

The house on the hill with the view of the valley has since nestled back into its lush gardens. The rains that came after the fires washed a cover of green regrowth over the bush, although the blackened trunks of burnt trees are still clearly in view. Memory of the fires will fade in time, both from the bush and from the people of the valley. But the story that is held in the bones of the Houstons' house might leave a message for the future: fire will come.

Melted plumbing fittings. (From the collection of John and Margaret Houston)

John and Margaret Houston's house, February 2011.

Erin-Marie O'Neill and John Brand

Erin-Marie O'Neill and John Brand had been living in their new home for not quite 10 months when it burnt to the ground, late on the evening of 7 February 2009. On the day of the fires they had executed their 'fire plan', including having blankets and buckets standing by. After being on high alert for most of the day, they popped out to the supermarket in Yarra Glen, only a 10-minute drive away, in the afternoon. It was from the shopping centre carpark that they could see the massive smoke pall forming above them: clearly a very large fire was heading towards the valley. Realising that their house would be under threat, they immediately headed back, driving north along Steels Creek Road. By the time they were halfway home, the fire had flared behind them, surrounding them on all sides. Houses were alight, the bush was ablaze and they were cut off from their property. After a terrifying retreat through smoke and flames, dodging fallen trees, and flying embers in almost zero visibility, with asphyxiated birds falling from the sky around them, they made it back to Yarra Glen and safety.

Erin-Marie and John's house before the fires. (From the collection of John Brand and Erin-Marie O'Neill)

The house they had been trying to return to was a cosy timber bungalow on the creek flats near the top end of the valley, surrounded by a billabong and 5 acres of grapevines. Known, in true Steels Creek style, as 'the Mullens' old place' for its previous dearly loved owners, the house was renowned for its beautiful garden, designed by the artist Christine Mullen and her husband Chris Grikscheit. The rambling flowerbeds, dotted with sculptures, and formal (highly productive) vegetable garden, wove between mature trees, and spread out across the 20-acre property. On one side of the house, a vineyard of pinot noir grapevines ran in rows from the road to the creek. On the other, a lazy elbow of the stream ambled through mature bush, past the French style garden sheds, before splaying out in an ornamental dam.

When they first saw the property John and Erin-Marie knew they had found something special. They were living in a small apartment in the heart of Melbourne but, having recently married, were looking for a change. They also knew that the suburbs were not for them; it was either the middle of the city or the rural fringe. The couple both had jobs that allowed them to communicate with their colleagues via the internet – telecommuting – so they had no need to be physically present in an office. Liberated by their working conditions, they were free to investigate options within a two-hour radius of Melbourne. After living in a vibrant cultural precinct for so long, however, they were not naïve about leaving their inner-city life for a country idyll. The key to their choice, they knew, would be finding a community of people with whom they felt a connection. Steels Creek was that community.

For this city couple, the early months of living in the valley were filled with learning about the vineyard. Growing 5 acres of pinot noir grapes is a significant undertaking and, with no experience in the field, they had a lot to catch up on. Their first tasks were to learn about pruning, spraying, tying, fertilising and irrigating and how each step affects the fruit. Manipulating subtle variations in flavour is the art of grape growing and in the initial months John and Erin-Marie were conducting their first experiments. By February 2009 their crop had been tested for sugar content and had returned promising results. After almost accidently irrigating at exactly the right time, they had arrived at a perfectly ripe and densely flavoured grape – one of the few crops of pinot noir successfully grown to maturity in the valley for that year. Having invested so much of their money, time and energy in their new venture, they were planning for their first harvest in mid February. It was an exciting moment.

While they were learning about the fine art of viticulture, they also had a massive garden to attend to, as well as a house to furnish and decorate. For the first time as a couple, they finally had the space to consolidate their possessions. The house was soon filled with their merged art collections, mementoes from travels, family heirlooms and valuable antiques. What didn't find a place in the house found a spot in the roomy sheds. The dust was finally settling for the newest members of the Steels Creek community and their rural life was taking shape. The moment was not to last.

The remains of the house, February 2009.
(From the collection of John Brand and Erin-Marie O'Neill)

John and Erin-Marie's house didn't burn down until quite late on the night of Black Saturday, well after most of the drama was over. A neighbour reported that they saw only the sheds ablaze after the fire front went through. The house survived until around 11 pm. Being on the creek flat and in primarily open grassland, the house was not, ironically, in a high bushfire danger zone and had easily survived the firestorm that wrought such massive destruction in other parts of the valley. But with red-hot embers in the burnt bush still pulsing in the wake of the fire front, it took only a puff of breeze for flames to flare. Grass wicked the fire along the ground; the flames found purchase in the timber buildings and over the course of the night, every possession that John and Erin-Marie owned either melted or turned to ash.

In contemporary Australia, it is not a common experience to own nothing more than the clothes you stand up in. The objects with which we construct our daily lives remain largely unnoticed while they are in use: the bread knife, the vacuum cleaner, the bath towel, the Tupperware containers. When they are missing, the role they play in smoothing our path becomes painfully apparent. For people who have lost everything through bushfire, there is often an unexpected twist in the experience. Research has shown, not surprisingly, that there is deep grief at the loss of important possessions, particularly those associated with memories of loved ones (such as wedding and baby photos as well as heirlooms that signify deep bonds with the past): the loss of more mundane objects, however, although traumatic, is often also experienced as a liberation, a clearing out of not only accumulated unwanted possessions but of ideas about what is needed to make life rich. The research also shows that the experience of losing everything influences the design decisions people make when it comes to rebuilding their house. Without particular possessions to accommodate, the designer is free to address more intangible ideas about space, light and flow. Architects reported to researchers that people who rebuilt after bushfires were more interested in building ecologically sustainable houses than fireproof houses. The emphasis was not necessarily on mitigating risk but rather on the connection being made between heat, drought, fire and climate change.[15]

When Erin-Marie and John sat down to brief their architect, they had a list of qualities that addressed exactly those elements. As Erin-Marie recalls, 'When we were designing the house I think the architect almost forgot that we didn't have anything. He asked us is there anything to include? I guess they build walls to the size of people's sideboards and things like that. We said no, we don't have any furniture. Our art collection is gone so we don't really need many walls.' Instead they presented him with a list of qualities that they felt were important. These included: passive heating and cooling; a feeling of freedom; a light environmental footprint; an abundance of natural light; and perhaps most importantly, that the views from the windows become a feature of the interior. As Erin-Marie explains, 'The fences and the gardens all burnt down and we now have views we didn't have before. The vistas are completely different. We want that to be part of our house. We want the outside, the surrounds, to be present with us inside.' Suddenly geography was an element of the architecture in a way that wasn't possible when the property was defined by developed ornamental gardens and mature growth bush.

That doesn't mean that the past wasn't important in their design. One of the most significant losses they experienced was of JB's music studio and vinyl collection, and Erin-Marie's piano. The antique upright grand had survived a journey from Germany in 1906. Erin-Marie's Nanna had taught students on it for 34 years. Her mum had done likewise before Erin-Marie herself had learnt to play on it. Suddenly, after more than a century of life in Australia, all that remained of the beautiful old instrument was the frame. Although they told the architect that they had no furniture to accommodate, they paused to consider: even though in essence it was 'gone', the remnants of the piano were important for their sense of connection to family and to music; perhaps they should somehow include it in their planning. On the other hand, they didn't want to create a homage to the fires. The delicate balance between

Erin-Marie plays the piano for her Nanna in Steels Creek before the fires.
(From the collection of John Brand and Erin-Marie O'Neill)

---

15 MacKenzie A (2011) *Keeping Ahead of the Joneses: The Incompatibility of Urban Environmental Efficiency and Development Practices in Suburbs Undergoing Renewal.* University of Canberra, ACT, State of Australian Cities conference, December, 2011.

a meaningful relationship to the past and the honouring of loss was struck when they decided to incorporate the burnt frame into their house as a design feature. Most moving was their insistence that the house be designed around the burnt concrete fish tank. The goldfish which miraculously survived the fires were a precious sign of life in the immediate aftermath of the blaze. Their continued presence in the new design was not negotiable.

Piano frame. (From the collection of John Brand and Erin-Marie O'Neill)

If finding themselves suddenly homeless was not an experience John and Erin-Marie were anticipating, neither was the news that they were expecting a baby. The decision to rebuild or sell-up had been complex before the birth of their son. The arrival of Henry, while they were still homeless, added a whole new dimension. With the added complexity of accommodating the future needs of a small child, they sifted through every option, weighing up the economics as well as social and cultural factors. It was not an easy equation. Erin-Marie explains, 'What we perhaps didn't realise when we came up here was that we bought a house and a vineyard. We thought we were buying a house with a vineyard but it was a lot more complicated than that. Of course the grapes all burnt just before they were due to be harvested. Because we have never received any income from them, we were not considered to be primary producers, and we weren't eligible for any government assistance. So that threw another spanner in the works.' Rebuilding is also expensive, more so than the option of renovating an existing property. At every turn they asked themselves, 'Are we doing the right thing?' Erin-Marie is frank when she admits to the agonising decision making process: 'There's no such thing as the right thing. What we realised is that there's no ideal solution. Even this isn't ideal, to be honest. But this is the best option. It comes down to us doing the best we can with the resources we have and how we want to live.' Ultimately, their decision to stay came back to the original reason for their move to Steels Creek. 'We talked to a couple of real estate agents and we may have basically broken even if we'd sold the land. That was our second option. The reason we didn't do that was because we couldn't work out where else we'd live. We really did think, where would we find a community like this, with these fantastic people? Once you've got to know the people you're a little bit tied in. You don't want to leave just 'cause of the fire. Community gets under your skin.'

This house on the creek flats, with its long views and natural light, is a symbol of more than survival. Its connection to the geography is a distinctive architectural response to the fires. John is reflective about this shift in perspective: 'We bought the place because we loved the artists' eye and how the landscape could be worked with to make something beautiful … Then suddenly, out of the fire, that has changed. Now with the rebuild, we're not trying to protect ourselves from the landscape, ironically we're trying to embed ourselves in it and feel part of it,' he explains. As the building settles into the charred foundations of its predecessor and the gardens grow up around it, it will hold in place the story of John and Erin-Marie's decision to commit to these people and this place. Another iteration of Steels Creek has found form.

The new house, April 2012. (From the collection of John Brand and Erin-Marie O'Neill)

The schoolhouses

When Dave Gormly and Sally Ferres chose to make their new home from two disused demountable schoolrooms joined by a central walkway, they were following a venerable Steels Creek architectural tradition: to make intelligent use of what is to hand.

Having lost their home in the fires, Dave and Sally were offered an old schoolroom, along with many of their neighbours, as emergency accommodation. The idea was simple but brilliantly conceived by Lynden McNamara of BRB-Modular in Bendigo. The paddock full of disused demountable schoolrooms is a well-known landmark along the Calder Highway for those travelling regularly between Melbourne and Bendigo. Moved by the plight of people who had lost their homes, Lynden saw the opportunity: disused buildings on one side of the mountains, people without housing on the other. His professional resources of heavy-duty moving

Demountable rooms – free to anyone who needed accommodation.
(From the collection of Dave Gormly and Sally Ferres)

equipment could provide the means to connect the two. This generous and clever impulse saw him offer the buildings to the Kinglake community in the first instance. Still shattered by their devastating loss, however, they were not yet ready to administer such a scheme.

In Steels Creek it was a different story. Craig and Eva Matthews had spent the three days before Black Saturday moving from their house in Melbourne's inner west to their property in the valley. They had owned the land for three years, coming up on weekends to stay in their half-converted shed and a caravan, but had found no time to get to know their neighbours before the fires hit. Although their shed survived, they were deeply moved to find themselves surrounded by people who had lost everything. Craig heard from a colleague in Kinglake about a chap offering to transport schoolhouses into areas where people had been left homeless. Concerned about his unknown neighbours, Craig rang Lynden to tell him that there was a need for temporary housing in Steels Creek and to ask if he could help. Lynden was happy to supply schoolhouses for free, delivered for free, to as many people needed them.

The Steels Creek grapevine swung into action. Craig and his neighbour Edd Williams helped coordinate a list of people who were interested. The Yarra Ranges Shire adapted their planning permissions process to accommodate the scheme. The ball was ready to roll.

Sally and Dave's place. (Photograph by James Calder)

Craig worked with his excavation equipment to clear access tracks to house sites and the schoolrooms mounted on trailers followed close behind. The volunteer team of Lynden, Craig, Edd and the truck drivers who tickled and prodded the buildings into place, often in difficult locations, were universally praised for their forbearance. If Craig hadn't known his neighbours beforehand, two weeks on an excavator helping people clear debris from their building sites turned strangers into instant friends.

While the schoolrooms were delivered free of any charges, it wasn't guaranteed they wouldn't be eccentric. One family was amused to find that theirs came with a sink, a blackboard and a school dress code. Another had previously been a computer room with carpet, an air conditioner and lots of power points. Others had classic schoolyard graffiti etched into the woodwork. Andrew Chapman was pretty sure theirs was from Yarra Glen: one of his younger visitors recognised it as the room used for detention and refused to go inside. The family still holds it in great affection, even though they have rebuilt. Edd and Amanda Williams were camping on their property before their schoolhouse arrived. Amanda was sleeping in her daughter's car. '[When they] arrived, each one on two trucks, they were put together and erected wherever we wanted on our properties. Each room was different so we all had something to start with. We spent about $20 000 to connect it to power and water and set it up as a temporary home.' At 6 squares each, all of them were large enough to fashion into multi-roomed homes with space for sleeping, cooking and living. People

had dry, light, airy accommodation on their own property instantly. Recipients of the buildings reported that of all the assistance they were offered in the wake of the fires, the schoolhouses were by far the most useful.

While most people used their schoolroom for temporary accommodation during the rebuilding process, Sally and Dave took it one step further. Inspired by the usefulness of the recycled building, they decided to purchase another and to use the two as the basis for their new home.

This ingenious adaptation of two ideas – the ephemeral house and the recycled house – is a truly local response to the fires. There is no question that the house is ephemeral: it is not a place you would choose to shelter in a firestorm and in bushfire the size of that which hit in 2009, this house would not survive. That in itself is a safety message. If you lived here you'd leave early, no question about it, which is one of the safest decisions you can make. Equally, it might last 60 or 70 years. Made out of what was to hand, this home is a light, comfortable, stylish modern version of the bush hut and a clever interpretation of emergency housing. And it didn't cost a fortune.

As the 21st century houses of Steels Creek rise to stand in the ashes of their predecessors, these schoolhouses, while they remain, tell the story of intelligence, adaptation and of practical generosity: architectural testament to the spirit of Steels Creek.

Stylish and comfortable – a perfect contemporary 'bush' home. (Photograph by James Calder)

Graham and Angie Lloyd

Like so many in the Steels Creek community, Graham and Angie Lloyd, heading in the general direction of retirement, had been looking for a 'lifestyle' block when they found their 12 acres on Steels Creek Road in July 2008. One of their criteria when looking for a place was that the house shouldn't be in the middle of the bush and wouldn't be particularly threatened by fire. The block they settled on was just the right size and the house, although quirky,

The Lloyd family home before and after February 7, 2009. (From the collection of Angie and Graham Lloyd)

was perfect for their purposes, with room enough for family and friends to visit and large windows looking out over the view. Originally a Merchant Builders farmhouse, the 38-year-old building had had a cedar weatherboard extension added sometime in the early 1990s. Far from being surrounded by trees, the brick and timber house was flanked by grazed paddocks front and back, exactly what they needed for their gardens, horses and chickens.

Not long after they moved to Steels Creek, the Lloyds went to a CFA meeting to seek advice about what precautions they needed to take to protect the house in the event of bushfire. Positioned low on the slope of the Yarra Ridge escarpment that formed the east boundary of the Kinglake National Park, the house was considered a low fire risk. Taking into account the history of fire in the area, the topography of their block and the openness of their paddocks, the CFA advised them that a fire would likely come out of the National Park to their north and move down the slope. Because it would be travelling downhill, the flames would slow and the radiant heat would be above the house. The flames would hit the open space of their empty paddocks leaving them plenty of time to get away. All in all, they had a good chance of defending their house, should it ever come to that. With this advice in mind, the Lloyds' installed some basic firefighting equipment and developed a fire plan.

On Saturday 7 February 2009 Graham's son Greg, his girlfriend Melanee Hermocilla, and her brother Jaeson, were house-sitting for Graham and Angie who were holidaying in Canberra; with temperatures in the mid 40s, the animals and gardens needed attention and the three young people

had anticipated a relaxing weekend in the countryside looking after the chooks and spending time together. The blistering hot air had initially folded in around them but by late afternoon Greg reported to his sister on the phone that a cool change had blown in and the temperature had dropped to something much more pleasant. What he didn't know was that the wind change was also blowing a massive fire front up the valley. Before the three friends could muster any attempt to fight the fire, the cars in the shed were alight and the house was full of smoke. Coming not from above as predicted, but below, flames quickly engulfed the house leaving no escape route. Two days later a senior constable of the disaster victim identification team found the bodies of Greg, Melanee and Jaeson in the region of the ruins that had previously been the bathroom.

As Graham and Angie were grieving the loss of the young people, the question of whether to rebuild or not was becoming pressing. They had been offered temporary accommodation in the city but they needed to make decisions about their future. As they weighed up their options, they both agreed that their strong affection for the community of the valley was an important consideration. Greg had also loved the place and had often talked of buying a property in the area himself. Partly as a memorial to him and partly because they felt they belonged there, they decided to return to their property and start again.

As so many people who were devastated by the fires report, the Lloyds had a complicated response to their enormous loss. Graham found that 'It was

The new house. (From the collection of Angie and Graham Lloyd)

The new house with upgraded fire fighting equipment. (From the collection of Angie and Graham Lloyd)

a strange experience losing everything you own. You realise how little any of it mattered.' When it came to thinking about what to rebuild, the lack of attachment to any possessions became their guide. The Lloyds explained:

The house that we were building had to serve a purpose. We weren't trying to find a house we would fall in love with, we wanted a house that would fit the lifestyle that we want to have. So we just worked out what that was and what we wanted. And then we walked in [to the builders] and said okay, this is what we want, what have you got? And they said yes we've got this.' We went 'that's very nice.' It was as simple as that. It wasn't a case of 'we're in a bad way, oh we can't be bothered, pick that one.' It was actually as soon as we walked in we knew.

The design they chose was a perfect fit. The size, the shape, the big windows, the open plan – the house struck them immediately as 'home'. The decision took no more than half an hour.

Choosing the plan, however, was not the end of the story. This time, building from scratch, they were in a position to include well-planned firefighting systems, although exactly what they would consist of was tragically hard won knowledge. One of the observations made during the Black Saturday Royal Commission enquiry into the deaths of Greg, Melanee, and Jaeson was that they had died in what was effectively a house fire that followed the passage of the bushfire. Trapped in the building, they were unable to get out onto burnt ground that may have, in other circumstances, provided an escape route. The terrible irony is that on seeking permission to rebuild, Graham and Angie's property was classified as being in almost the lowest fire risk category in the area, requiring them to meet minimal mandatory building requirements. They understandably chose to exceed those limits substantially.

The first level of defence they installed was a fail-proof water supply. Although their previous water storage capacity had been generous, with a 50 000-litre concrete tank for the house and two smaller 5000-litre tanks catching run-off from the garage for the gardens, the supply was powered by a single electric pressure pump with no firefighting pump or generator. When the fire hit, water was of course the immediate concern. Not knowing the fire drill, Greg phoned his father to ask for help. 'I said fill up the bath with water. Well the power was down, and because the power was down, none of the water pumps worked. No access to water.' That was a failure of design that Graham and Angie were determined would not be replicated. This time they have an extensive system that covers both the house roof and the garden.

That's why we've got a generator that could probably charge half this valley. The idea was to put a tank up the top, behind the barn, that would then gravity feed water to the house, so no matter what happened we would have water.

While thinking of their own safety, they were also concerned to provide important infrastructure to the community in case of a future fire emergency. The 20 000-litre tank at the top of the driveway fills from the dam, which gives instant access to an extensive water supply. The tank is also fitted with a CFA connection of which the local brigades are now aware. In future, any fire truck will be able to draw on the considerable dam supply through the tank in an emergency. In installing the tank with CFA fittings, the Lloyds were concerned to acquit the money they received from donations to maximum possible effect. Graham explains that they considered it 'the least we could do [to] put in as much protection as we could, so that's what we did. The Rotary Club of Williamstown, they donated the money for that tank.'

The 'wine cellar' with extra features. (From the collection of Angie and Graham Lloyd)

During their enquiry the Royal Commission commented on the bathroom of the Lloyds' property proving an inadequate refuge for the young people to shelter in. In this respect their house was not alone. None of the homes in which people died on Black Saturday had any type of 'last resort' retreat available. For no discernible reason, the fire refuge as a domestic architectural feature is not an idea that has taken off in Australia, even in the enormously dangerous 'flume' zone of the south-east corner. Having no 'last resort' refuge was a fatal failure on Black Saturday, not just for Greg and his friends but for all of the 173 men, women and children who perished in the fires. Where once the 'dugout' was a common feature of bush camps and settlements, today they are rarely considered.

When Angie and Graham turned their attention to building a fire refuge, they hit an inexplicably obstructive bureaucratic response. Graham found the experience hugely frustrating. 'In three years no-one will tell us what the requirements [for a fire bunker] are. I've contacted the CFA, they've put me on to Victoria Building. I've sent emails. I've made phone calls. No-one's got back to me. We still don't know.' Despite the lack of advice available and the unwillingness of the State's building and fire authorities to assist, they put together ideas from the internet and came up with their own plan. The bunker is now tucked into the slope above the house. Based on an adapted underground concrete water tank, the room is buried on all but one side. It has a fire-rated door on the exposed wall and the air vent at the back has a metal panel that can be screwed down to prevent smoke coming in. Angie is satisfied that it would do in an absolute emergency.

It's a reasonable size so it's reasonable the amount of air inside. It's quite spacious so if you had to be in there for 15 minutes or half an hour, whatever, you should have sufficient air. Again you don't know because let's be honest, you don't [know] what the circumstances are going to be, how much smoke's going to get in there and so on.

Despite her determination to have a last resort refuge as part of their domestic infrastructure, Angie refuses to be drawn into seeing her new home as framed by disaster.

Healing Day, 15 March 2009. (From the collection of Angie and Graham Lloyd)

The thought of having [the bunker] just in case of something God awful like that happening again, to me was negative. I always wanted to have a wine cellar, so now I've got one. And it's starting to get built over, I've got some creepers now growing over the front of it. By the time it's finished it'll blend beautifully into the hill and be a nice feature of the place. And I do keep wine in it. So we've put a wine cellar out the back, or from the council's point of view a concrete shed. It's kind of just the insurance that you don't ever expect to need because it's the final backup after all the other backups. But we don't ever plan on getting to that point.

While Angie and Graham were coming to terms with their loss in the first few weeks after the fire, many people asked them what they could do to help. Angie quickly realised that their wider network of friends and family were also struggling to understand what had happened and that they desperately needed to participate in some way. They decided to hold a 'healing day' at the property, where anyone who wanted could join them in helping to clear debris from the house site. Angie explains:

[We] recognised that this wasn't just about us … So I sent out an email to our close friends and said this is what we're doing, if anyone would like to come here's a suggestion: you'll need protective gear, it is filthy, you'll need gloves, you'll need spades, you'll need shovels, you'll need whatever. That email probably went out to 20 people who sent it on to their friends … 120 turned up on the day. There were other people who were very disappointed not being able to come along. One guy actually drove all the way from Sydney and he wasn't even someone that we knew. But he just wanted so desperately to do something.

It was important to both of them that it was a healing day not just for them but for the land. Angie found that clearing the debris was cathartic. 'Getting rid of what was broken and what was nasty and the horrible memories – it was great'. Burnt and broken fencing was pulled up, trees removed and cut into logs, bricks from the old house were cleaned and stacked and, most importantly for Angie, a new garden bed was made. For her, a growing garden signified new life, 'because you plant something for what it will look like in the future'. The healing day was the beginning of 'life after the fires'. As she reported 'It was a pretty special sort of a day. I really believe strongly that if you create the space for people to be great, they usually are. It was a fabulous, fabulous memory'.

The healing day might have been the beginning of their life 'after the fires', but the hard work of dealing with the loss of Graham's son Greg and his friends Melanee and Jaeson has only just begun. Rebuilding on the old site has been an important milestone in that process, although not one that everybody understands. For Graham, the decision was clear: 'Some people said to me, how can you possibly go back there with your son who died and his girlfriend and brother, and my response to them was, well how can I not go back?' For Angie, the land itself is the connection: 'Because Greg died here, we felt closer to him here. Like it's not in a morbid way. Thinking of Greg does make me sad but thinking of him actually makes me happy too because he was such a gorgeous young man. And I feel closer to him here'.

The new house is starting to settle into its surrounds as the gardens grow, the wine cellar begins to fill and friends and family spend happy times around the barbeque again. But the house with its gravity feed water supply, extensive sprinkler system and concrete fire refuge tells a story that will last well into the future: fire will come again and it will be dangerous. Understand the threat and be ready to survive.

Graham	*I want to say, we cannot thank the unknown people in Australia and overseas enough, 'cos we had people from overseas donating and helping as well, we cannot thank them enough. If it wasn't for them it would have been so, so much harder. We cannot thank them enough. Wherever we go, particularly if it's interstate we let them know, 'cos people ask, oh how're you going? Yeah, going well. Did the money get through to you? Yes it did. 'Cos we're hearing all sorts of awful stories about the money. No, it all got through, everything, thank you very much. So you know if we can … everybody in the world, thank everybody for what they did. I wish I could write them all a letter personally, but I can't.*
Angie	*… it's a very … it is an incredibly special valley and incredibly special people in it.*
Graham	*Some are weird though.*
Angie	*Oh we're all weird, that's why we fit in.*[16]

16   Angie and Graham Lloyd interviewed by Tom Griffiths, Steels Creek, 17 February 2012. See also Royal Commission Hearings, 17 May 2010.

Bushfire art

Richard was very traumatised by the fire, by the loss of friends, and he had smoke inhalation. Making the gate was his way of coming to terms with it. He gathered tools from friends' sheds [that were burnt] and welded them together.

Margaret McLoughlin

Gate by Richard McLoughlin. (Photo: James Calder)

Artists at work

As well as rebuilding their lives after Black Saturday, locals responded to the fire by painting, drawing, sculpting, welding, stitching and writing. Art, always important for many in the valley, became a way of working through their emotions and of coming to terms with what had happened.

(From top left) Jane Calder quilting; Robyn Henchel talks about her painting (see her art on p. 158); Malcolm Calder presents his 'Tangled Leaves' (see also p. 54); Ray Dahlstrom and Ivan Filsell (see their art on pp. 92-3, 154-55, 157).

(From left) Christine Mullen, Margaret Houston, Christine Hansen, Jane Calder, Robyn Henchel and Pam Verhoeven gather in November 2010 to talk about their artwork since the fire. (Photos: Ingereth Macfarlane)

Christine Mullen's book of 'Fire' inspired by Robert Frost's poem 'Fire and Ice' that begins 'Some say the world will end in fire ...'

All that was left was wire…

After the 39 fire all that was left on our farm was wire and I thought to myself, well, you can't farm wire. That's when I joined the army.

Fred Sadlier

… steel girders and machinery were twisted by heat as if they had been of fine wire

Judge Leonard Stretton 1939

We tried to contain and control everything with wire. Wire created extraordinary forms in the landscape. When the buildings and fences were gone you could see the beautiful organic contours of the land and wonder why we divided it up into small rectangles.

Christine Mullen 2009

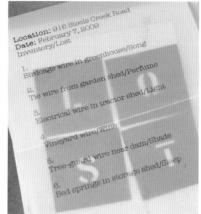

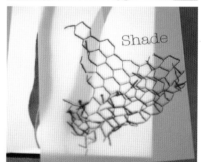

Box of wire: Christine Mullen created an inventory of wire collected from the site of her former home, destroyed by fire. In the old cash box used at the Community Centre, she gathered burnt wire from greenhouse, sheds, vineyard and dam.

Artists (clockwise from top left): Deva Daricha, Christine Mullen, Margaret McLoughlin, Chris Griksheit, Ivan Filsell, Margaret Brewster, Jane Calder.

Artists (clockwise from top left): Margaret Houston, Margaret McLoughlin, Malcolm Calder, Noel Nicolson, Margaret Houston, Robyn Henchel, Ray Dahlstrom.

Nicole and Stephen Beecroft and their children Samantha and Ellie escaped from the flames but lost their home.

My children painted what they imagined their Nana [Dorothy Barber] would have seen while she was trapped in her house during the fire. They know what they saw; they didn't know what she saw. … The girls were sitting in the back of the car as we were leaving through the flames, one on each side. One later drew the images of the burnt side that she could see, and the other chose to draw the green of before the fire. The whole time we were driving out, the girls were looking out the windows watching their world burn, while we were concentrating on the road to get out safely. The children saw everything. There was not much left for the imagination, apart from their Nana's experience, and the demons are in the imagination. I feel they have a better grip on the whole tragedy than others who didn't see.

The girls lost a lot of their animals in the fire. They've been drawing them ever since.

Nicole Beecroft

Samantha, Ellie and Nicole with some of their craftwork completed since the fire. Nicole says: 'I need cushions, oven-mitts, bathmats. I'm replacing things.'

Samantha's diorama of her home in the bush, before and after the fire, completed as a school project.

Archaeology

Eighteen months after the fires, I was told about a woman who had always been fascinated by archaeology. Her burnt out house site presented an opportunity to forage for treasures. She was still sifting then and is probably still sifting. We, too, sifted through ashes for treasures. We were surprised that some things we thought may have survived were untraceable; others were changed beyond recognition, while some things were only slightly affected.

The blue head was made by our son, Michael, when he was at school in Year 8. After the fire it had a red colour that was not there previously and it had acquired a glass eye.

Unlike the woman who is fascinated by archaeology, we won't find any more treasures. Grocon did a great job clearing our site. I'm glad that we were able to retrieve some items, but in the end it's not the items that matter, it's people and memories. Bron Dahlstrom

Aftershock

Watching our Steels Creek Road house burn down was a surreal experience which I find difficult to talk about. People assume that I must have gone through a traumatic and horrific experience, but this was not the case. At the time it seemed serene watching a house that we built and had occupied for 25 years burn down. In some ways standing in front of the burning building, with the clothes I was wearing my only belonging(s), was a cleansing experience. I wanted to capture the peace I felt immediately after the fires; hence the use of subdued colours.

I couldn't see the fire coming. The hills behind the house blocked any vision of the flames that were about to descend. Still unaware of the oncoming peril, it was the continual changing colours of the clouds that held my attention. Pink, white grey, black, yellow, red, brown. No wind disturbing the crowns of the yellow box and manna gum. And the embers, tumbling softly down. Nothing fierce in the softly spinning small fragments of charred bark and leaf. Still unaware of the destruction that they would bring.

The horror of February 7 came later – newspaper and television images of the ferocity of the fire and the massive amount of carbon being emitted into the atmosphere. When I returned to 375 Steels Creek Road and saw what was left of our 66 acres of bush – powdered ash and blackened charred landscape – I tried to imagine what it would have been like to be in the middle of that raging inferno. What was the carbon footprint and how did I ever walk away?

Just so you know how hot it was – I dug roast potatoes the next day. Ray Dahlstrom

I never bought black paint until 2009 and I went through tubes and tubes of it.

Robyn Henchel

Robyn's art tells a story of recovery. She says that her first painting after the fire had her fenced in by the tragedy. The black trees were 'like prison bars'.

Then in 2010 she introduced her first colour. Over the next year or two there was an explosion of colour. 'This is what I see now … like a filigree, these gorgeous colours, the orange of the moss. I have burst into colour.'

Like everyone I was at first devastated. Apart from the immediate house and garden the 10 acres of bush we own had disappeared. Thick ash covered the ground, there was no undergrowth, familiar bush tracks no longer existed and you could see contours in the land never revealed before.

After the shock, despair and malaise began to decline and when it was safe to do so, I started exploring the bush. Within two weeks I found the first new growth on the small grass trees. What I also discovered was an amazing beauty. If you looked beyond the destruction there was a new palette of colours and incredible shapes and textures. The tones of black, grey and white against the blue of a summer sky were striking and the white marks left on the bark of burnt trees inspired an almost Aboriginal style of painting to emerge in my work. That year I went through tubes and tubes of black paint. My paintings became a lot more abstract and less self-conscious. I took a lot of photos and would paint particular images that when completed could initially overwhelm me with sadness. Sometimes the paintings seemed to paint themselves.

I am really thankful that I had a creative outlet that I am convinced helped my personal recovery.

I started to use colour again in 2010 and whilst black still features in my landscapes, colour is definitely the focus. One looks out onto grey and black dead trees that form a tracery of branches against a constantly changing sky. Below the trees there is an understorey of new eucalypts that are so thick they form a maze as you walk around the reinstated bush tracks. Each new eucalypt is crowned with vivid bright green and pink new growth and below this is a mass of grasses.

I feel fortunate to live where I do, to have survived Black Saturday and to be an eyewitness to nature's amazing recovery. It is hard to believe that a few years on the bush is lush, filled with birds, butterflies and the sound of frogs.

Remembering

Tom Griffiths

The most shocking fact about Black Saturday is that people died where they thought they were safest, where they were *told* they would be safest. Of the 173 people killed on Black Saturday, two-thirds of them died in their own homes. Of those, a quarter died sheltering in the bath. There were relatively few injured survivors: the annihilation was total. The day after brought an awful stillness and silence.

We should have seen this coming. We *did* see this coming. Yet we failed to save lives. Have we still not lived long enough?

The Bureau of Meteorology predicted the conditions superbly. The Victorian Premier, John Brumby, issued a public warning. Fire experts knew that people would die that day. History repeated itself with uncanny precision. Yet the shock was, and still is, immense. It is the death toll – and the way people died at home and without warning – that horrifies us.

The Victorian Emergency Services Commissioner, Bruce Esplin, woke at 6 am on Black Saturday with, as he put it, 'this feeling of dread'.[1] It was probably no accident that he used the word 'dread', the same word Leonard Stretton

---

1   Details of the progress of the fire in this chapter are drawn from Stewart C and Perkin C (2009) How the battle for Victoria was fought and lost. *The Weekend Australian*, 14–15 February, pp. 1, 6–7. In this chapter I have drawn on some of my earlier reflections on Black Saturday which were published in *History Australia* **6**(2) 2009 ('"An unnatural disaster"? Remembering and forgetting bushfire'), *Inside Story*, 8 October 2011 ('From the ashes') and *Griffith Review* ('The language of catastrophe'), as well as my Eldershaw Lecture for the Tasmanian Historical Research Association in the Hobart Town Hall on 11 October 2011.

used to describe the feelings of bush workers in the summer of 1938–39 as the dry undergrowth crunched ominously under their boots. Esplin was very familiar with Stretton's report. On that morning of 7 February 2009, an hour or two's drive to the north and east of Melbourne thousands of families awoke to a fierce day and instinctively stayed indoors. Most had probably heard the warnings the day before. Many knew that, in the event of fire, if they were not going to stay and defend their homes, then they should leave early. But when, exactly, was *early*? It was still too early for most that Saturday morning – there were no reports of fires close by, and anyway it was better to stay at home than to travel in such conditions. The Premier had encouraged people to stay indoors if they could. 'Everyone was fatigued by the hot days', recalled one Steels Creek survivor who lost his home. 'It produced complacency. The whole family was having a siesta. Tarps were strung up on the windows, the air-con was on. The tarps were flapping, I couldn't sleep.' Later that day, without time for any further decisions, people with fire plans were ambushed by a monster. 'Many times before we've seen smoke', they remembered. Another recalled: 'We've stood on our front lawn and watched fires on the ridge. This was not a fire, but a tsunami, a wave of gas not so much of flames.' 'Normally you see a cloud', observed a survivor. 'This one was so hot it was white – like a giant cumulus. We never saw flames. It was incandescent.' At Woods Point in 1939, old residents initially ignored the huge pall of smoke coming over the north-eastern hill; they had seen it often enough before. Within an hour their town was incinerated. At Marysville in 2009, tourists were innocently captivated by a photogenic magenta 'thundercloud' billowing above the town; they blithely played around the swimming pool and took snaps of the strange phenomenon above them. It was about to descend on them 'like an atomic bomb'. The survivors spoke constantly of the immense speed and noise of the fires. 'No-one could have stopped it', they said.[2]

Emergency Service chiefs in what was called 'the war room' in Melbourne, equipped with the best communication technology, were also overtaken by the speed and ferocity of the event. By early afternoon on that Saturday, fire authorities in that 'war room' were anxious but buoyant. So far as they knew, fire activity was limited. Yet the Kilmore East fire was already alight and rampaging. Dozens of people died in the next few hours. Bruce Esplin recalled: 'We were sure that the fires were taking houses at that stage but we had no idea they were taking lives.' The close association in this fire between houses and death had not yet been made – but the official 'Stay or Go' policy had this very alliance between people and their homes at its core. Kinglake West was consumed, then Strathewen, St Andrews, Kinglake, Steels Creek, Calignee and Flowerdale, all were overwhelmed. By 6 pm, with the southerly change sweeping across central Victoria, there was still no confirmation in the 'war room' that any lives had been lost. Driven by the new southerly winds, fire bore down on Marysville and vaporised it. Esplin heard the news six hours later. When he went to bed at 1.30 am the official death toll stood at 14.

---

2   Most of these quotes are from survivors of the Black Saturday fire at Steels Creek. The Woods Point story was told by Gerald Alipius Carey to the 1939 Royal Commission and can be found in Moira Fahy's online documentary about Black Friday (http://www.abc.net.au/blackfriday), and the Marysville account is by Legge K (2009) Blithe oblivion. *The Weekend Australian Magazine*, 7–8 March, pp. 18–21.

Forgetting

Extraordinary as Black Saturday was, it had happened before, as this book has emphasised. There are enough Black days in modern Australian history to fill up a week several times over – Black Sundays, Mondays, Tuesdays, Thursdays, Fridays and Saturdays – and a Red Tuesday too, plus the grim irony of an Ash Wednesday. Yet we keep being taken unawares. We seem unable to carry the memory of the ferocity of nature from one event to the next. One thing that we never seem to learn from history is that nature can overwhelm culture, that some of the fires that roar out of the Australian bush are unstoppable. It seems to go against the grain of our humanity to admit that fact, no matter how severe are the lessons of history.

There is something personal about fire, something frighteningly irrational and ultimately beyond our comprehension. It roars out of the bush and out of our nightmares. Reporting of bushfire constantly portrays it as a monster. In 1919 and 1926, houses were 'swallowed' and people were 'caught between the jaws of the flame'. Fire 'with its appetite whetted … sought more victims, and fiercely attacked', and 'with each change of wind … made a thrust towards the township, threatening to lick up the scattered homes on the fringe'.[3]

Bushfire makes its victims feel hunted down and its survivors toyed with. *Why did the fire destroy the house next door and leave mine unscathed?* As one bushfire survivor has confessed: 'I felt as if the fire knew me'. A book about the 2003 Canberra fires takes as its title a child's question: *How did the fire know we lived here?*[4] The great international fire historian Stephen Pyne keeps telling us that fire 'isn't listening to the rhetoric, the research, or the parliamentary resolutions. It doesn't feel our pain. It doesn't care. It just is.'[5] Why does he need to assure us of this?

---

3   *Healesville and Yarra Glen Guardian*, 27 February 1926, p. 3, 6 February 1926, p. 1; *Lilydale Express*, 21 February 1919, p. 3.

4   Matthews S (Ed.) (2003) *How did the fire know we lived here? Canberra's bushfires January 2003*. Ginninderra Press in association with Pirion, Charnwood, ACT. I am grateful to Karen Downing for this reference, and to Robert Kenny for his insights into the experience of fire.

5   Pyne SJ (2006) *The Still-Burning Bush*. Scribe Publications, Melbourne, p. 9.

Fire is the genie of the bush ready to escape, 'the red steer' jumping the fence and running amok, the rampant beast that can savage and kill. Instead of the sprites, elves and wood nymphs that populated the forest folklore of the northern hemisphere, Australian colonists found that their bush harboured a rather different creature. As poet and essayist Les Murray put it, the 'gum forest's smoky ambience reminds us that the presiding spirit who sleeps at

its unreachable heart is not troll or goblin, but an orange-yellow monster who forbids any lasting intrusion there, any buildings or other human constructions.'[6]

Forgetting begins earlier than we know. It is accepted wisdom that there is always a heightened awareness of the danger of fire after a tragic event such as Black Saturday, but as the years pass, complacency sets in and the memory of the horror dims. That's a pattern of gradually declining memory that we recognise and understand. But there is another more troubling psychological and cultural pattern that we can observe at work in the months immediately after a great fire. The forgetting of the recurrent power of nature is immediately and insidiously embedded in the ways we describe and respond to disaster. Our sympathy for the victims of bushfire, the surge of public financial support and the political imperative to rebuild as swiftly as possible conspire to constrain cultural adaptation. Such sacrifice of life cries out for meaning and for a kind of unbending resolution in the face of nature. There is often an emotional need, as people return and rebuild, to deny the 'naturalness' and therefore the inevitable recurrence of the event. Black Saturday, we quickly reassured ourselves, was 'unique', 'unprecedented', 'unnatural' – and it was a 'disaster'. We must never let it happen again! Culture can – and *will* – triumph over nature, we declare.

'An unnatural disaster' was the phrase that the Secretary of the Marysville Historical Society, Mary Kenealy, used to make sense of Black Saturday. As the deadly bushfire approached their town, she and her husband Reg heroically

6   Murray L (1985) *The Australian Year*. Angus & Robertson, Sydney, p. 9.

tried to save their community's precious historical collection. They rushed to their Society's resource centre, frantically packed the most significant material in a trailer, and drove it home to their carport. They covered the photos and manuscripts with a tarpaulin that they kept moist as the radiant heat of the firestorm escalated. The Kenealys stayed with the papers as long as they could, and then they fled. The resource centre, their home and the trailer of treasures were all incinerated, and Reg and Mary, escaping at the last minute in their car, were nearly hit by a fallen tree. They miraculously survived – although many of their friends didn't know that for days. Their town, famous for its grace and historic charm, was vaporised.[7]

People escaping their homes in the face of fire reach first for the photo albums. So too does a threatened community strive to preserve the material fabric of its corporate life's memories – and later its surviving stories. History is no luxury or afterthought at such times. It is a primal sob of desperation; it is an instinct and a hunger. When Mary Kenealy was finally allowed back with other residents to see the devastation of her township from the windows of a bus, she started writing. She awoke in exile early the next morning, sat up in bed and found herself writing a sequel to her 2006 history of Marysville, *The High Way to Heaven*. She said that she already had a theme and perhaps a title for the next volume: *Razed/Raised*. 'Razed by an unnatural disaster; raised by love, hope, faith and a powerful community spirit', she explained.[8]

Mary Kenealy seems to have chosen that adjective 'unnatural' instinctively. It is a description that goes to the heart of the debates about this great fire. Many commentators immediately insisted that the 2009 fires were 'unprecedented'. They erupted at the end of a record heatwave and there seems little doubt that this was a fire exacerbated by climate change. It was no 'ordinary' fire; it was a firestorm. It could not be fought. It did not burn; it cremated. And in Marysville, as well as in other places, the awful spectre of arson seems to have had grim substance. The smoking ruins of the township were declared a 'crime scene' for weeks. The sinister barriers of police tape seemed to confirm the impression that the event was unnatural.

Yet such a word turns its back upon the very nature that has sustained these forest communities. Marysville, even more than Steels Creek, is close to, and economically supported by, the forests of ash, where firestorms are endemic. So however understandable it is to distinguish the disaster as 'unnatural' – however human is that impulse and however reasonable it is in the aftermath of shock – it is dangerous to do so. Such a fire will come again, with or without climate change, with or without arsonists. The whole environment of the Yarra Ranges conspires to utilise a spark, any spark, on such a day. And it will be impossible to fight. Reaching for that adjective 'unnatural' is the beginning of our forgetting.

There is an irresistible tendency to use language that describes bushfire almost wholly in terms of tragedy and destruction. Not only do we talk in crisis language: we also use military metaphors and comparisons – partly because, in the face of an awesome natural force, they offer some comforting human agency. The response to the call to fight the 1962 fires 'was worthy of

7   Turnbull G (2009) Bushfire situation in AEHS region. *Newsletter of the Association of Eastern Historical Societies Inc.* no. 1, February 2009.
8   Lamperd R (2009) History razed, but not lost. *Herald Sun* (Melbourne), 16 February, p. 11.

the highest traditions of our race', declared the *Lilydale Express*. 'All in all it was a magnificent effort which reflected the will-to-win of the Australian people'. It was a baptism of fire, a rite of passage: 'the fun-loving youth of our district turn into men overnight'.[9] And in 2009, as we've seen, we referred to the Melbourne fire authorities as hunkered down in 'the war room'. We revere the heroism of the firefighters and compare them to Anzacs, linking the domestic fire front to the nation's grand narratives of overseas war. At the national memorial service to the victims of Black Saturday Prime Minister Kevin Rudd spoke of 'a new army of heroes where the yellow helmet evokes the same reverence as the slouch hat of old'.[10] Refuges are 'dugouts' and people who are not firefighters are 'civilians'. We describe forests as *destroyed*, even if they are highly evolved to burn. We call great fires 'holocausts'. We yearn for better technology to suppress the fire front. We bomb the flames with water. We talk of hitting the fires hard and hitting them fast. Arsonists are 'terrorists'. The fires are 'a threat to national security'.

Heroism, in such a culture, is defined as staying and fighting. Leaving your home early might be seen to be cowardly, a kind of betrayal of community. At the memorial service many speakers, in honouring the dead and their heroism, were unwittingly cornering another generation. 'Courage,' Kevin Rudd declared, 'is a firefighter standing before the gates of hell unflinching, unyielding with eyes of steel saying, "Here I stand, I can do no other."'[11] Yet one of the triumphs of the Black Saturday tragedy was that not a single firefighter died on the day.[12] In the face of that horror fire officers knew when to retreat.

It must have been a shocking decision to make but it was the right one, or the death toll would have been much higher. We all have to learn better when to retreat – and we have to find a word other than 'retreat'. These military metaphors make us believe that we can and must *beat* fire, somehow. Yet our challenging task as Australians is to learn to live with it.

Mandy Martin, Wanderers in the Desert of the Real; Aftermath, *2009, oil, pigment, ochre on linen 100 × 150 cm.*

---

9   *Lilydale Express*, 19 January, 26 January, 12 February 1962.

10   Rudd K (2009) Nation shows its courage and compassion. *Age*, 23 February.

11   Rudd K, 'Nation shows its courage and compassion'.

12   However, David Balfour, an ACT firefighter, was crushed by a falling mountain ash tree when doing 'mop-up' work near Marysville 10 days after the firestorm.

Words

The other terrible 7 February in our country's history of Black Days was Black Tuesday 1967 in Tasmania. On that day Roger Wettenhall, a political scientist, was very surprised to find himself fighting bushfire in his own suburban front garden and backyard. Wettenhall instantly became interested in the way his society had responded to the crisis, how its political and firefighting institutions had stood up to the test. 'Very few of us in fact saw a fire brigade that day,' he recalled. 'Hobart was grossly ill-prepared.'[13] He began researching and writing a detailed study of Black Tuesday, which was published in 1975 and called *Bushfire Disaster: An Australian Community in Crisis*.

Drawing on the international scholarly literature of disaster, Wettenhall argued that the most significant thing about disaster is not the suffering or loss, nor our capacity to recover from adversity, but rather the 'extraordinary optimism, common to most people, that we ourselves will not be stricken; or that, if indeed disaster should strike, it will not recur'. The other insight that illuminated his case study of disaster was drawn from the American social scientist Kenneth Boulding, who observed that humans have always tended to regard disaster control as 'a problem in engineering rather than in sociology'. So Wettenhall noted of Tasmania: 'Though officialdom had taken some pains to analyse certain material elements in these [disaster] experiences and had thereby effected improvements in, for example, firefighting and flood-protection techniques and resources, the broader social issues had received scant attention.'[14]

These, then, were the two insights that shaped Wettenhall's study: that people, through optimism and forgetfulness, generally fail to believe that disaster will recur, and that understanding the social origins and impact of disaster nearly always comes second to addressing its material or physical dimensions.[15]

Roger Wettenhall's important book set out to make sense of how he came to be fighting a 'fire hurricane' in his suburban yard, and it was also an attempt to generate an Australian sociology of disaster. What kinds of writing and reflection have the 2009 fires so far produced?

It is four winters now since the Black Saturday bushfire brought its terror. Soaking rains have inspired grass and forest growth that is both heartening and frightening. New houses have sprouted like lignotubers where their predecessors were gutted. Other homes – razed, flattened and cleared – are haunting absences. The Royal Commission, which cranked through 155 days of evidence, has finished and reported, and already its recommendations have dust on them. After the last two summers of disasters – floods, cyclones, earthquakes and tsunamis – bushfire survivors are sharing their experience with new victims of nature's wilfulness. And from the ashes, from the regrowth and renewal, from the pain and the horror, there now comes some wisdom.

13   Wettenhall RL (1975) *Bushfire Disaster: An Australian Community in Crisis*. Angus & Robertson, Sydney, pp. v, xiii.
14   Wettenhall RL, *Bushfire Disaster*, pp. 65–66.
15   For Roger Wettenhall's further reflections on this area of policy, see his 'Crises and natural disasters: a review of two schools of study drawing on Australian wildfire experience', in *Public Organization Review* **9**, 2009, pp. 247–261.

Slashes of bright green fire moss three months after Black Saturday.

The most enduring wisdom forged by the Black Friday 1939 fire came in the form of Judge Leonard Stretton's Royal Commission Report. It was also the greatest literary legacy of that fire. There were no other published words about Black Friday that compared with the biblical power of Stretton's report.[16] It was celebrated not only as a political statement but also as literature. For many

years it was a prescribed text in Victorian Matriculation English, and politicians and fire managers consulted it. In 2002–03, as the Alps burned, Victorian Premier Steve Bracks borrowed Stretton's 1939 report from the Parliamentary Library for his weekend reading. Bruce Esplin, head of the Victorian bushfire inquiry of 2003, said he could feel Judge Stretton looking over his shoulder. Stretton's words still resonate with poetic and political power: he was fearless.

Justice Bernard Teague's Royal Commission Report into the most recent Black Saturday fires is earnest and thorough but too careful and comprehensive to make memorable literature. It is becoming clear that Black Saturday is shaping a different and more diverse literary legacy. Black Friday 1939, followed so quickly by years of world war, did not generate any notable books, although it did induce lifelong trauma, become embedded in folklore and language, and seed political and bureaucratic reform. But Black Saturday 2009 is quickly germinating a forest of impressive writing: perceptive essays by John van Tiggelen, Robert Manne, Robert Hillman; Danielle Clode's *A Future in Flames*, Roger Franklin's *Inferno*, Peter Stanley's *Black Saturday at Steels Creek*. And Adrian Hyland's *Kinglake-350* and Karen Kissane's *Worst of Days*, two impressive books that focus on the Kilmore East fire and together offer a powerful portrait of how a disaster unfolds – and of its political and emotional aftermath.[17]

Adrian Hyland's *Kinglake-350* takes us into the world of the Kinglake Ranges as they are about to be consumed by the fire that is storming unheralded

16   Stretton LEB (1939) *Report of the Royal Commission into the Causes of and Measures Taken to Prevent the Bushfires of Jan. 1939*. Government Printer, Melbourne.

17   van Tiggelen J (2009) Comment. *The Monthly*, March, pp. 8–12; Manne R (2009) Why we weren't warned: the Victorian bushfires and the royal commission. *The Monthly*, July, pp. 22–35; Hillman R (2009) The fire this time. *Griffith Review* no. 25, spring, pp. 201–208; Clode D (2010) *A Future in Flames*. Melbourne University Press, Melbourne; Franklin R (2009) *Inferno: The day Victoria burned*. Slattery Media Group, Melbourne; Stanley P (2013, forthcoming) *Black Saturday at Steels Creek*. Scribe, Melbourne; Hyland A (2011) *Kinglake-350*. Text Publishing, Melbourne; Kissane K (2010) *Worst of Days: Inside the Black Saturday Firestorm*. Hachette Australia, Sydney.

towards them. The story's main character is Acting Sergeant Roger Wood of the Kinglake Police, and his call sign is Kinglake-350. We follow him from dawn on 7 February; learn what he is doing, thinking and fearing; and feel the drama of Black Saturday explode around him. Through him we meet the people of Kinglake, and gain a visceral sense of the caprice and violence of a firestorm in the ash range. Adrian Hyland knows these people because he lives with them. This is superb non-fiction writing: dramatic, full of tension, deeply researched, true.

Karen Kissane's *Worst of Days*, published before the Royal Commission's final report, has its foundation in her work as the Melbourne *Age*'s chief reporter on the commission. Like Hyland, Kissane structured her compelling narrative around selected individuals, but her book is also a piece of sustained investigative journalism. Daily immersion in the hearings and evidence of the Royal Commission is transmuted into history and literature with perspective and punch. She seems determined to find a voice that is stronger and tougher than the 'disapproving puzzlement' and 'neutral, non-condemnatory tones' of the commission's interim report. As Kissane puts it, 'the commission's [interim] report reflected the evidence before it, in which so many emergency workers and bureaucrats using phrases right out of Sir Humphrey Appleby's mouth had smoothly declined to take responsibility for any failures: it was not their job, or they were working at a higher level, or their underlings should have told them if there was a problem.'[18]

The historian, speechwriter and brilliant analyst of language Don Watson has described Black Saturday as 'the day words fell short'.[19] Seven months after the fires he reflected on the evidence that fire managers were giving to the Royal Commission about what they called 'communication': 'One CFA manager described the business of telling the public as "messaging"; "communicating the likely impact"; "to communicate the degree of the circumstance"; providing "precise complex fire behaviour information"; "to communicate more effectively in a timely manner not just that it is a bad day, but other factors as well". He spoke of his task as "value-adding" and "populating the document". He and other managers talked a good deal about "learnings", "big learnings" and even "huge learnings"'.

Watson concluded: 'It was not that they did not do their very, very best. More likely, when it came to telling people what they had to know, their management training made their best inadequate. Telling people requires language whose meaning is plain and unmistakable. Managerial language is never this.'[20]

Karen Kissane and Adrian Hyland have thrown off the blanket of bureaucratic blandness and set out to distil a very different kind of language of disaster. They have tapped into what Robert Hillman called 'the vernacular of Australian catastrophe': spare, vivid storytelling, full of people doing things, full of verbs, full of agency and responsibility. Hillman, who lives near Warburton

18   Kissane K, *Worst of Days*, p. 292.
19   Watson D (2009) Vital lessons from the day words fell short. *Age*, 19 September 2009.
20   Fire scholars can be just as bad. Here is T. Andrew Au in 2011 in the *Australian Journal of Emergency Management* **26**(3, July), 20–29, analysing, of all things, *communication* on Black Saturday: 'Our results point to lack of efficiencies in the network connectedness, which is an enabler of coordination efficiency. An enduring solution will necessitate synergy between qualified people, well designed processes, and enabling technology in order to break down seemingly complex coordination challenges.'

and found himself caught within a horseshoe of the fire, was spellbound through the night of 7 February by radio accounts from survivors, by 'the terrible beauty of tales in which there is no exaggeration, no sentimentality', and which were as gripping in their brevity 'as the verses of an ancient ballad'. He confessed that he became 'absorbed by the way in which disaster restores the vigour of language', just as the fire cauterised the forest itself, ridding it of excess and reducing it to a weirdly beautiful austerity. Hillman felt that the best memorials to the victims of Black Saturday would not be the secular and religious services imbued with hyperbole and cliché, but the 'unrehearsed narratives' of those who escaped.[21] Peter Stanley has worked with the people of Steels Creek to capture those narratives for this valley.

Adrian Hyland's book feeds off the lean poetry of such unrehearsed narratives by weaving a tapestry of stories in the present tense. This enables us to see that, even as people are overwhelmed by an unbelievable force of nature, there are still tiny interstices of time and space in which they can exercise their will, understanding and wisdom. Inevitability and luck are two dominant metaphors for explaining and coping with disaster, and they play large roles in Hyland's narrative, too, but his focus on people doing things – especially the policemen at the centre of the drama – reveals how individuals can still make a difference in such a crisis. Hyland creates room for heroes without diminishing our understanding of the ecological and climatic forces within which they were trapped.

There are heroes in *Worst of Days* too, but also more death and inevitability. Having sat through the Royal Commission hearings, Karen Kissane understandably grapples more directly with the 'managerial language' of the bureaucrats, and its consequences. She finds that 'the evidence suggests the CFA was resistant to making warnings as high a priority as firefighting: its operational focus has been on trucks and crews rather than towns and residents'. The commissioners concurred, and in their final report recommended that 'fire agencies … attach the same value to community education and warnings as they do to fire-suppression operations'.[22] Let us hope that this recommendation is followed. It will involve deep structural and philosophical change. We live in a society that is presented with daily reports of the Nikkei Index but learns nothing of the Fire Danger Index.

Kissane's book offered a sustained analysis of the systemic failures on Black Saturday and, in particular, an impressive demolition of the 'Prepare, Stay and Defend or Leave Early' policy, abbreviated to 'Stay or Go' and often distilled in the official mantra that 'People save houses. Houses save people'. Kissane declared this policy 'the final victim of Black Saturday'.

21   Hillman R, 'The fire this time', pp. 201–208.
22   The Hon. Bernard Teague AO, Ronald McLeod AM and Susan Pascoe AM, *2009 Victorian Bushfires Royal Commission Final Report*, volume 2, p. 3.

'Stay or Go'

In the week after Black Saturday I argued on *Inside Story* and in *The Age* that the 'Stay or Go' policy was a death sentence in these Victorian mountain communities on a 40-something-degree day of high winds after a prolonged heatwave and a long drought.[23] Although the policy has guided people well in most areas of Australia and has demonstrably saved lives and homes, it misled people in this distinctively deadly fire region to believe that they could defend an ordinary home in the face of an unimaginable force. Clearing the backyard, cleaning the gutters and installing a better water pump cannot save a home in the path of a surging torrent of explosive gas.

The policy – through its enshrinement of the defendable home in any circumstances – also implicitly sanctioned the gradual abandonment of community fire refuges over recent decades. As we explored in Chapter 3, the fire refuge dugout was a distinctive cultural response to the history of fire in these tall Victorian forests, and developed in the era of bush sawmilling in the early 20th century. Few dugouts were built in other forest regions of Australia, but those that did exist in these Victorian ranges saved dozens of lives in 1939.[24] It seems that they might now be making a comeback. Some of the people who lost homes on Black Saturday have decided to rebuild with fire refuges on their properties. The Black Saturday Royal Commission recommended the designation of community refuges in high-risk areas and,

in October 2011, the building of the state's first official fire refuge in the region was announced.

I believe that the 'Stay or Go' policy also underpinned the lack of warnings issued by authorities to local residents about the movement of the fire front. The Royal Commission rightly gave sustained attention to the failure of warning systems on Black Saturday. It is one of the most haunting aspects of this tragedy – the weird official paralysis that prevented the issuing of warnings to those communities known to be in the path of the firestorm. In one case an accurate warning was not issued from the Kilmore Incident Control Centre (ICC) because the fax machine was not operating. But it was not uploaded to the CFA website either.[25] Specific warnings were drafted and ready to be sent out several hours before deaths occurred in Steels Creek. Kevin Tolhurst's fire mapping team in the Integrated Emergency Control Centre produced predictive maps of the fire before 1 pm, but they were not issued. At about 2.40 pm on Black Saturday, the Deputy Incident Controller at Kangaroo Ground, Rocky Barca, predicted that the fire would reach Kinglake, Kinglake West, Strathewen, St Andrews, Steels Creek, Flowerdale, Humevale and surrounding towns and areas.[26] But the message was not sent because Kangaroo Ground was not the designated ICC for the fire.[27] Even as the day's events unfolded, the Kilmore ICC was acknowledged as dysfunctional by those

---

23   Griffiths T (2009) We have still not lived long enough. *Inside Story*, 16 February. http://inside.org.au/we-have-still-not-lived-long-enough/, and *Age*, Insight section, 21 February 2009.

24   Peter Evans, 'Refuge from fire: sawmill dugouts in Victoria', in John Dargavel (Ed.) *Australia's Ever-Changing Forests III*, Centre for Resource and Environmental Studies, Australian National University, Canberra, 1997, pp. 216–228.

25   Teague *et al., 2009 Victorian Bushfires Royal Commission Final Report*, volume 1, p. 80.

26   Teague *et al., 2009 Victorian Bushfires Royal Commission Final Report*, volume 1, p. 78.

27   Teague *et al., 2009 Victorian Bushfires Royal Commission Final Report*, volume 1, p. 81.

trying to work with it. Although the firestorm moved quickly into the domain of the Kangaroo Ground ICC during the afternoon of 7 February, it was not until 5.42 am the following day that Kangaroo Ground was granted 'control' of the fire. In Marysville, too, 'those who saw the signs tried to warn the public but, there again, the links fell apart in the chain somewhere higher up.'[28]

We have to analyse this paralysis; not just its surface manifestations, but also its culture. The most senior authorities knew the power and path of the fire, although those in the new Integrated Emergency Coordination Centre in Melbourne were surprisingly insulated from the detail. Staff in the Kilmore and Kangaroo Ground Incident Control Centres also knew where the fire was heading. But people in the region, people directly in the path of the firestorm who were relying on their radios, TVs and internet to keep them informed, did not know. Power company SP Ausnet was warned that its assets were under threat at Kinglake but residents of the town were told nothing.[29]

In an article in *The Monthly* in July 2009, Robert Manne, who survived the fire in Cottlesbridge due to 'a mere fluke of wind', analysed the evidence then presented to the Teague Royal Commission in an attempt to understand why so few warnings were issued by authorities on the day.[30] He was perplexed and angry that people in the path of the fire were not given the benefit of the latest information about the fire front. He and his wife were ready to leave should they learn that the fire was coming their way. They followed the news of the Kilmore East fire and heard that Wandong had come under attack. They knew that this meant that the fire had jumped the Hume Highway and, worryingly, had reached the dense, tall forests of Mount Disappointment. Then they heard nothing more – other than, about 5 pm, 'an unearthly roar' which they later thought may have been the firestorm descending on St Andrews, 6 km to their north. Soon afterwards, the wind changed. They were astonished that, in the information age when 'people across the globe learn within minutes if a plane crashes or a volcano erupts', they were left for 10 hours knowing 'nothing whatever about a monster fire a few kilometres away'.

While residents remained uninformed during the afternoon, roadblocks were put in place in some of the threatened areas. In several reported cases, locals were allowed through only if they were returning to their homes. As Robert Manne reported, police ordered several residents to return to their homes in Pine Ridge Road in Kinglake West where they perished shortly afterwards. Evacuation was being discouraged but returning home was being facilitated, even in some cases demanded. Threat warnings remained suppressed by the bureaucracy.

I think there is a system here – a logic – that we need to recognise. It is connected to the 'Stay or Go' policy. Sinister as all these actions seem, they were consistent with a fear of late evacuations and a faith in the safety of the home. How did such a policy evolve and become so strong by 2009?

---

28   Cowan J (2009) CFA 'in a mess' on Black Saturday. *The Drum*, 22 June.

29   Kissane K, *Worst of Days*, p. 294.

30   Manne R (2009) Why we weren't warned: the Victorian bushfires and the Royal Commission. *The Monthly*, July, pp. 22–35.

There had been earlier intimations of the policy. Foresters Alan McArthur and Phil Cheney had moved towards it in their report on the Hobart 1967 fire (although it was not remarked that half the 'civilian' deaths occurred in or near homes).[31] Then in 1969, Australians were shocked when 17 people died in or escaping from their cars when a grassfire swept across a major highway surrounded by open paddocks, at Lara between Melbourne and Geelong. Travelling through a fire was clearly perilous, even in modern cars and on a broad, multi-lane highway.

But it was the Ash Wednesday firestorm of 1983 that prompted a clear change of policy. Ash Wednesday, which was like Black Friday in intensity if not in range, confronted the modern firefighting community with the limits of its capacity and technology. It also brought tragedy. Seventeen firefighters died that day, most of them next to their well-equipped tankers on a forest road in Upper Beaconsfield when the wind changed and the firestorm swept over them. The experience forced changes in firefighting strategies and philosophies. How to save firefighters from sacrificing themselves? And how to get the community more engaged and better informed? The 'Stay or Go' policy, which had been developing quietly since 1967, began to be articulated more clearly from 1983 and evolved from these good questions.

Ash Wednesday initiated a sensible search for 'shared responsibility' and 'community self-reliance' in firefighting. People had again been reminded that some firestorms cannot be stopped or even hindered, even by the most sophisticated of firefighting forces. On Ash Wednesday, the CFA observed that 'normal fire prevention had little effect … on the forward spread of the fire'.[32] It was also apparent that during such an event, the CFA would not be able to offer protection to every home. Therefore homeowners should not expect firefighting assistance and would need to make their own decisions and preparations. Fire expert David Packham, an early advocate of the 'Stay or Go' policy, survived the Ash Wednesday fire by successfully defending his own home at Upper Beaconsfield.[33] It was a close call, but seemed to confirm the proposition that people were safer to stay put than to evacuate late, especially with the tragic example of superbly equipped and trained firefighters caught on the road nearby. This was the crux of the policy: that it was far safer for citizens to be in their own homes, prepared and ready to fight, than it was to be on the roads.

That same year, 1983, Packham spoke often of his experience, arguing strongly that, because radiation was such a killer, 'The safest place in a bushfire is inside a building!' He added that 'the very best way to make sure a house does not burn down in a bushfire is to have somebody in it!'[34] The philosophy that 'People save houses. Houses save people' was beginning to crystallise. Since radiant heat was a major killer and houses were most at risk from ember attack, the partnership made sense. The policy was founded on an assumption that a fire front takes only minutes to pass, a belief challenged by many

31   McArthur AG and Cheney NP (1967) *Report on the Southern Tasmanian Bushfires of 7 February 1967*. Forestry Commission Tasmania, Government Printer, Hobart.

32   Quoted in Krusel N and Petris SN (1992) *A Study of Civilian Deaths in the 1983 Ash Wednesday Bushfires Victoria, Australia*. CFA Occasional Paper, no. 1, CFA, Melbourne, p. 4.

33   Packham D (1984) Planning for a hot time. *All Journal*, February, pp. 29–32; Pyne SJ, *Burning Bush*, pp. 416–419.

34   Packham D, 'Planning for a hot time', p. 30.

accounts on Black Saturday. Packham argued against 'the irrational evacuation mentality that is sweeping some of the bureaucracies of this State [Victoria]'. Compulsory evacuation in such situations was a policy often applied overseas, especially in the United States, and so there was some patriotic pride in the development of a libertarian 'Australian approach' of community self-reliance. These feelings encouraged the aspiration to articulate a *national* policy.

Ash Wednesday 1983, like Black Tuesday 1967, confirmed that the new frontier of fire in Australia was the expanding 'interface' between the city and the bush.

A generation after sawmilling communities were withdrawn from the bush following the recommendations of Judge Stretton in 1939, communities were again being established deep in the forests. This was always going to be a dangerous amalgam, as it had been before, but it was made even more so by the fashion for native gardens that developed strongly from the 1970s. This proliferating zone – spreading along winding bush roads – called for new protective measures and different firefighting philosophies. If a 'shared responsibility' was called for, then research was needed into why people die in bushfires.

In 2005, fire scientists John Handmer and Amalie Tibbits reviewed the development of the 'Stay or Go' policy.[35] Their account shows a strengthening articulation, especially since Ash Wednesday, of faith in the safety of the home – always in contrast to late evacuation. As Handmer and Tibbits said of Ash Wednesday, 'the clearest lesson from these fires was that late evacuation is dangerous'. So the policy focus turned to the people who stayed and to ways of empowering them. New fires and the enquiries they generated interacted with the policy position, generally confirming it. The Sydney fires of 1994, the 2002–03 fires of Victoria and the ACT, and the Eyre Peninsula fires in South Australia in 2005 seemed to show that people who stayed and actively defended their homes had a better chance of survival than late evacuees. On the Eyre Peninsula, eight of the nine deaths occurred in cars. However, the Dandenong Ranges fires of 1997, where all three victims died in their homes, seemed to challenge the policy, especially as none of their neighbours perished despite some very late evacuations. But Handmer and Tibbits argued that the policy remained sound because the people who died in 1997 were 'adopting a more passive sheltering strategy' rather than actively defending.

This last argument – where contrary evidence was explained away and an 'ideal' form of behaviour was expected – revealed a worrying tendency in the scholarship supporting the 'Stay or Go' policy. We can see how this is embedded in one of the foundation pieces of research on which the policy depended, a 1984 article entitled 'Fight or Flee?' by forestry academics Andrew Wilson and Ian Ferguson published in *Australian Forestry*. Wilson and Ferguson analysed the experience of Mt Macedon residents in the Ash Wednesday fires and concluded that 'able-bodied residents who are threatened by a bushfire should remain in their houses. Their chances of survival are excellent, and 90 percent can expect to save their houses'.[36] The authors were careful to stress that these findings emerged from a fire that was 'at, or near, the maximum intensity possible'. This article is constantly cited as proving that, on Ash

---

35   Handmer J and Tibbits A (2005) Is staying at home the safest option during bushfires? Historical evidence for an Australian approach. *Environmental Hazards* **6**, 81–91.

36   Wilson AAG and Ferguson IS (1984) Fight or flee? A case study of the Mount Macedon bushfire. *Australian Forestry* **47**(4), 230–236.

Wednesday, 'twice as many deaths occurred in vehicles or out in the open than inside houses'. But the death statistics are much more ambiguous than this suggests. The authors argued that of the 46 'civilian' deaths in Victoria on Ash Wednesday, only seven occurred in houses. But drawing on exactly the same statistics, it would be equally valid to say that of the 46 deaths, a third died defending their homes (15), a third died evacuating (18), and a third died firefighting in the open (13). Or we could say even more bluntly that five out of the six people who died at Mount Macedon that day were killed in or near their homes. In other words, for such an influential piece of research that is said to establish the relative safety of the home, the evidence is surprisingly inconclusive.

Of those five deaths in or near homes at Mt Macedon, Wilson and Ferguson argued that all the people were over 55, one was disabled and one lived in a steep, forested location exposed to a fully developed crown fire. 'In our opinion', argue the authors of all but the last death, 'able-bodied occupants would not have lost their lives.' Therefore: 'The results of this survey suggest that evacuation should not be undertaken lightly, if at all.' This is the same argument made of the home deaths in the 1997 Dandenong fires. Even the language of Wilson and Ferguson's article – 'Fight or Flee?' – was heavily weighted towards preferring the more noble, able-bodied defence of the home castle. Leaving early or late was contrastively labelled 'fleeing'.

Ash Wednesday confirmed the enduring bush wisdom that late evacuation in a bushfire is perilous. It also reminded us that many houses burn down after the fire front has passed. Therefore people can indeed save homes, and many did in Steels Creek on Black Saturday. But Ash Wednesday, contrary to accepted opinion, did not prove that homes will save people. And Black Saturday demolished the mantra completely.

What is evident from a short history of the 'Stay or Go' policy is that, as it settled in, its architects began to marginalise the evidence against it. Their policy was a utopian ideal, and for various reasons that scientists and managers were keen to explain, real life did not always live up to it. You needed the right kind of people, properly prepared and living in the right kind of houses, to make it come true. And it reduced the options available to people to a simple choice, and one which – with its language of 'fighting' and 'defending' and the prospect of saving one's home – was also implicitly presented as a moral decision. Moreover, as the 2009 Royal Commission was to find, 'The policy did not tell people they risked death and serious injury if they stayed to defend.'[37] By 2008 the CFA was preparing to address these flaws and contradictions. There was a growing acceptance that, while the policy was 'soundly based in evidence', there were problems of community understanding and 'implementation'.

What, then, is the sound evidence upon which the policy was based? A keystone retrospective rationale for the 'Stay or Go' policy was the research finding by Dr Katharine Haynes that 'the majority of civilian fatalities in bushfires between the commencement of written records and early 2008 occurred while victims attempted to flee the flames during late evacuation.'[38]

37   Teague *et al., 2009 Victorian Bushfires Royal Commission Final Report*, volume 2, p. 5.
38   Submission of the State of Victoria for the Interim Report, 1 July 2009, p. 21, in 'Transcript of Proceedings', 2009 Victorian Bushfires Royal Commission, Melbourne.

This finding remained unquestioned by the 2009 Royal Commission that called its lead author, Dr Haynes, to give evidence. Since it is such a crucial empirical foundation for the policy and was heavily relied upon by the Royal Commission and by fire and emergency services officers, it is worth scrutinising its use of evidence. Drawing on coronial records, Haynes investigated the history of Australian bushfire 'civilian' fatalities since 1900 and concluded that 'late evacuation is the most common activity at the time of death'.[39] But this finding only emerges from the historical data if you place in different categories those people who died inside their homes and those who died outside them while trying to defend them. If you make that distinction, then a large number of deaths are classified as 'outside' instead of 'defending the home'. This allows 'late evacuations' to emerge, by a small margin, as the 'most common activity at the time of death' (32%). But if you combine the people who died inside houses with those defending the property outside – all of whom it could be said were 'staying and defending their home' – then that becomes the major cause of death (35%). And over just the last 50 years, the proportion of deaths of people defending their properties increased to 39% compared to 29% for those evacuating late. Everyone accepts that late evacuations are perilous. But it appears that, even before Black Saturday, staying and defending could be described as the most dangerous choice a homeowner could make. After Black Saturday, of course, no matter how you read the statistics, that is definitely the case.

Haynes, like Handmer and Tibbits, and Wilson and Ferguson, also seeks to attribute deaths in houses to the capacity or behaviour of the people inside.

The victims 'were passively sheltering' or making 'meagre and unsuccessful attempts to defend'. Haynes goes so far as to argue that not one 'prepared' person out of the 552 'civilians' killed in bushfires since 1900 died while defending a 'defendable structure' – they either left too late, unwisely fought the fire outside their home, failed to fight when inside, or had a heart attack in the home when defending and therefore died 'not directly from the bushfire'. Thus the utopian policy is left intact, unsullied by messy human behaviour or imperfect human bodies.

Haynes' analysis is also unable to apply any discrimination to the process of evacuation. People sometimes leave late because the threat is much greater than they imagined or their house is about to burn, even if the initial decision they made was to stay and defend. Haynes categorises them as 'late evacuations'. What about the people found burned to death between their home and their car (which was nearby, already packed and had keys in it, thus following David Packham's sensible advice to those staying and defending to have a means of escape)?[40] When giving evidence before the Royal Commission, Haynes appeared to categorise them as 'late evacuations' although her published work may register them as 'outside the home'. Either way, they are again excluded from the definition of 'Inside defendable property'. Yet the art of defending a home is choosing when to protect yourself inside from the radiant heat and when to go outside to put out flames and embers. Those who evacuated early or 'just in time' – or, indeed, too late but miraculously survived – do not register in the data because only deaths are analysed. Thus successful evacuation is unmeasured. It is very

39   Haynes K, Handmer J, McAneney J, Tibbits A and Coates L (2010) Australian bushfire fatalities 1900–2008: exploring trends in relation to the 'Prepare, stay and defend or leave early' policy. *Environmental Science and Policy* **13**, 185–194. An earlier version of this research was made available to the Royal Commission.
40   Packham D, 'Planning for a hot time'.

surprising that the Royal Commission was led to believe that this was the only piece of historical research on this issue and that it accepted it without historical scrutiny.[41] Researching and writing good history is a demanding craft, and understanding the complexity of real life requires careful contextual analysis. It is not easily reduced to statistics. And statistics can be very misleading, especially when your sample size is 552 and draws on events spanning a century.

So this was the thinking – evident in both the research and management – that underpinned the relentless logic of the 'Stay or Go' policy. Robert Manne was right to ask in July 2009: 'Had a decision not to issue warnings in the circumstances of 7 February been taken?' His answer, and I agree with him, was 'Yes' – 'both a cumbersome bureaucratic structure and a peculiar ideological mindset had worked in combination to prevent the fire and emergency chiefs … from issuing warnings'.

The failure to issue warnings to communities in the path of the firestorm was partly due to error and bureaucratic paralysis, but it was also because of a conviction that late warnings would precipitate late evacuations, and that people are most vulnerable when in panicked flight. The logic of the policy was that, once the fire is on the move, it is best to keep people at home. Therefore warnings might seem to be a low priority; they might even seem dangerous.

And it's not just that people weren't warned. They were falsely reassured – by the policy; by the advisory literature, which made defending a home in this region on such a day seem a reasonable option; and by the slow, vague and misleading official information that was released about the fire front. Karen Kissane observes that at the same time as the 'Stay or Go' policy insisted people take on an adult responsibility for their fates, it 'also infantilised them by withholding key information'. Her analysis of 'the official mind' is devastating. 'While the CFA was arguing over who should run the Kilmore fire,' she writes, 'the fire came and went.'[42] In the public messages issued there was 'deadly oversight of the bleeding obvious'.[43] The defensive managerial language observed by Don Watson was doing its obstructive work.

Disturbingly, this defensive language has, at times, also been assertive in undermining local experience and observation. We have seen how people who live in the Yarra Ranges developed special words and phrases for the extreme fire behaviour they have repeatedly witnessed. But many fire scholars and professionals forgot the force of fire in tall, wet forests and began to doubt what people said they saw in 1851 or 1926 or 1939 or 1962 or 1983. According to this view, the unrehearsed narratives of survivors were actually exaggerated fictions or 'myths' that needed to be dispelled by calm professional education, fire science and 'the laws of physics'.[44] We are told by the fire professionals that, in the 1944 fires, houses did not simply 'explode' as people reported, and that in the 1967 fire 'most accounts of houses exploding can be disregarded'.

---

41 Commissioner McLeod was the only one to sense the problem when she asked 'So in a sense in your survey their deaths [people outside their homes] don't add any weight to whether it is better to leave early or whether it is better to stay because they haven't consciously made that choice? – Yes. ('Transcript of Proceedings', p. 458).

42 Kissane K, *Worst of Days*, p. 201.

43 Kissane K, *Worst of Days*, p. 38.

44 Schauble J (2008) Red steers and exploding houses: cultural interpretations of bushfire and community understanding. MA thesis, University of Melbourne, kindly made available by the author.

And that in the 1983 fire an 'extensive survey of houses in the Otway region of Victoria after Ash Wednesday debunked stories of "exploding houses"'.[45] As for Judge Stretton's famous account of exploding houses in his 1939 Royal Commission Report, John Handmer takes the trouble to interpolate that the judge's statement is 'not supported by quotes'. Stretton didn't need to quote because the descriptions are there in the two and a half thousand pages of testimony to his Royal Commission. John Nicholson, a former Director of Risk Management at the CFA, argued in 1994 that, 'To be effective, this community education process must actively seek to dispel myths about Australian wildfires, for example fire fronts do not move at such phenomenal speeds as sometimes reported in the popular press' – and of course he adds that houses don't explode.[46] If people believe that houses can actually explode – or that fire fronts can move surprisingly quickly – they might not stay in their homes during a firestorm. Handmer argues that, in rural areas, '"staying" has always been a likely choice of survival strategy' in bushfire. But the historical experience of Steels Creek in the first half of the 20th century contradicts this. Most people knew their homes weren't safe, and either escaped or dug desperately into the creek bank.

As recently as 2008 thoughtful fire officers – drawing narrowly on the science of grassfires – argued that there were no such phenomena as 'exploding houses' or 'firestorms' or 'fireballs', and that these were just the delirious words of people unfamiliar with fire. And they suggested that such untutored and emotive words also falsely implied that 'bushfire is something beyond human control'. Nothing shows the psychological blinkers of the 'Stay or Go' policy more powerfully than this professional disparagement of eyewitness accounts of fire in a distinctive forest. Dugouts and 'fireballs' were material and verbal evidence of local cultural adaptation, and yet both were abandoned and disparaged by authorities seeking universal solutions and national policies.

Because the research underlying the 'Stay or Go' policy remained unchallenged by the Black Saturday Royal Commission, the commissioners concluded that 'the central tenets' of the policy 'remain sound'. But their report did recommend major changes: a need for the policy to recognise variations in the severity of fires resulting from 'different topography, fuel loads and

Drawing by Michael Leunig, created on 18 February 2009 and published in the Saturday Age, *21 February 2009.*

---

45   Wilson AAG and Ferguson IS, 'Fight or flee?'; Handmer J and Tibbits A, 'Is staying at home the safest option during bushfires?'

46   Nicholson J, AFSM (1994) Mass evacuation: is total evacuation of a community threatened by wildfire a sound strategy? Paper presented to the Institution of Fire Engineers, New South Wales Branch, 1994 State Conference, Sydney, available at <www.communitysafety.com>.

weather conditions', and a need to resist the simplistic 'binary approach' of the policy. 'Realistic advice is unavoidably more complex and requires subtlety', argued the commissioners, and this would involve providing a greater range of practical options such as community refuges, bushfire shelters and evacuation. Community education would need to include the message that 'among the risks of staying to defend are death and serious injury'.

To live with periodic, recurrent firestorms, I think we need to develop a sensible fatalism. If people are going to live in the heart of the bush in the most dangerous fire region of the planet, then on the worst days a 'stay and defend' option is only realistic if your property has a secure fire refuge or bunker. Working out how to build safe, secure and affordable refuges on each vulnerable property is an appropriate challenge to the design and construction industries of the fire continent.

The blame game

In his closing reflection in *Kinglake-350* Adrian Hyland asks: 'So how does contemporary Australia respond to the dilemma of fire?' His answer: 'With lawyers.'[47] It is hard for a 'profession whose primary function is to find somebody guilty or innocent' not to be drawn into the blame game. But if there is blame to be assigned here, we all share in it. Hyland regrets 'the trophy-hunting convolutions that surrounded the Black Saturday Royal Commission', and the way barristers and journalists 'circled for the kill'. These distractions meant, he believed, 'that there was little attention left … for an examination of the nation's soul'.

The former Victorian Emergency Services Commissioner Bruce Esplin observed in a radio interview in August 2010 that a Royal Commission 'can be a very legal process and it can be a process that thereby stifles proper debate because people are concerned about the implications of what they may or may not say.'[48] Perhaps the commissioners themselves were frustrated by these constraints, for their final recommendation (no. 67) is that 'the state consider the development of legislation for the conduct of inquiries in Victoria – in particular, the conduct of Royal Commissions'.

The Black Saturday Royal Commission had some conspicuous strengths: it was consultative and exhaustive. It had the patience and grim determination to expose, in forensic detail, the bureaucratic absurdities. And it took very seriously its emotional and political commitment to the victims and their families – 'We have been conscious of your pain and loss throughout our work.' The commission made a priority of travelling to suffering communities for its initial consultation sessions, and shared its city proceedings with the general public through webcasts. It also convened special hearings into the circumstances of every death, sessions that were as much therapeutic as investigative. Family and friends of the deceased were welcomed, and invited to participate. Justice Teague explained to those present that it was 'a different kind of hearing', one that dispensed with some of the legal formalities and aimed 'to get the information we need but in a way that will save you having to be exposed to a great deal of detail'. This was part of the commission's very impressive commitment to 'securing the memories of the fires'.

47   Hyland A, *Kinglake-350*, p. 242.

48   Bruce Esplin, interview with Jon Faine (Melbourne ABC radio), 4 August 2010

The Black Saturday Royal Commission was less successful in guiding the adversarial legal style of the courtroom away from the pursuit of personal blame. At times – most notably in the cross-examination of the former Victorian Police Chief Christine Nixon, by senior counsel Rachel Doyle – the commission allowed its proceedings to be hijacked by another agenda. Stronger moral guidance from the commission to counsel and to the media might have engendered greater public attention to the significant systemic and cultural flaws it unearthed. The shocking point about Christine Nixon's whereabouts on the evening of 7 February is that, even if she had spent every second of that night in the newly established Integrated Emergency Coordination Centre ('the war room'), she wouldn't have known much more about the unfolding disaster than she did sitting in a North Melbourne pub.

Could Justice Teague have moderated the distracting media frenzy of blame? Possibly not. But it is worth recalling again that earlier Royal Commission in 1939 – admittedly a very different era in terms of media morals and power, but still an instructive example. Judge Leonard Stretton began proceedings with these words: 'I wish to make it clear at the outset that this is not an inquisitorial Commission. I do not represent any punitive or detection arm of the law; I am here merely to arrive at the broad causes of the recent fire disasters and to make recommendations later, if any suggest themselves to me, for future assistance. If any person feels embarrassed by being asked to give evidence, or if he feels that he may incriminate himself, he has only to say so, and he will be given the protection which the law affords him.'[49] Stretton constantly monitored and guided his proceedings to ensure the investigation of broad causes rather than individual blame. 'I want to get to the truth, but I do not want to embarrass anyone,' he explained again at his first country hearing, in Healesville. But he did not hesitate to excoriate the daily newspapers when they threatened his search for truth. He blasted them for their 'blackguardly lies' in reporting his commission and its witnesses, especially – he added with typical wit and mischief – 'that section of the press which is printed for the more unintelligent, who can absorb their news only in picture form apparently'.[50]

Ecological, local and historical thinking

On the sixth day of the Royal Commission hearings on 18 May 2009, Justice Bernard Teague was looking for the right noun to describe the bushfire of 7 February. Addressing Bruce Esplin, he said: 'One thing that strikes me is that the Australians appear not to have adopted the [American] word "mega fire" but it seems to me that either that expression or some other expression would be highly desirable … Are there adjectives that you otherwise use – extreme, catastrophic, ferocious, feral – are there any of those that would [mean] we don't have to adopt the Americanism?' Bruce Esplin agreed that a distinctive term was desirable but could not suggest an appropriate one: 'Whether "mega fire" or some other term, there needs to be some way that we can perhaps … get them to understand that this is something different.'[51]

---

49   Judge Leonard Stretton speaking at the opening of hearings at Healesville, February 1939, 'Transcript of evidence given before the Royal Commission to enquire into the causes and origins and other matters arising out of bush fires in Victoria during the month of January 1939', 3 volumes, Department of Primary Industries Library, Victoria.

50   Judge Stretton speaking at the opening of hearings at Noojee, 1 March 1939, in 'Transcript of evidence' (3 vols), Royal Commission into the 1939 fires.

51   'Transcript of Proceedings', 2009 Victorian Bushfires Royal Commission, Bruce Esplin, 18 May 2009, pp. 562–563.

We have suggested in this book that we use the word 'firestorm' to differentiate the ferocious and fatal recurrent fires of our history from other, more frequent bushfires. We need to recognise the difference because, as Karen Kissane put it in *Worst of Days*, 'some fires are so extraordinarily fast and intense that, in the face of their fury, even the best prepared and well-defended home is doomed to ashes'. I would add that they are not just 'some' fires, but specific types of firestorms in a particular region on predictable kinds of days. The Royal Commission went some way towards being more discriminatory about the variety of bushfire, weather, topography and ecology; but not far enough. There is still insufficient recognition of the distinctiveness of the fire region through which the Black Saturday firestorm moved so quickly. I find it astonishing that no vegetation map appears in the Royal Commission's interim or final reports. The forests enter the report mostly as 'fuel'. 'The natural environment,' the commissioners explain in their introduction, 'was heavily impacted.'[52] I can see Don Watson wincing.

The lack of a vegetation map in the Royal Commission report reminds us how difficult it is for humans, especially those charged with political analysis, to recognise the diverse agency of nature. The cover of the commission's *Interim Report* featured the work of a Kinglake artist depicting the signature tree of the fire region of Black Saturday: the mountain ash, *Eucalyptus regnans*. However, the artist represented this highly distinctive tree as a generic eucalypt. The drawings are botanically unobservant. The mountain ash has a tall unbranching trunk and a small, high, compact, tapering crown – quite the opposite of the wide-branching, spreading eucalypt invented by the artist and used by the Royal Commission to represent the firestorm. The mountain ash appears on the cover of the *Interim Report* as a standard burnt tree, not as a peculiar, distinct tree with a fatal talent. By what process does a key ecological and local insight become lost in the instinct to commemorate a general experience and perception of fire? The art on the cover had another purpose, of course – it was a moving, local expression of grief – but the point here is to observe that an ecological sensibility does not come easily to us, even when ecology holds a truth about a particular fire, even when the specific subject of study is that fire, and even when that ecological insight is possibly crucial to human survival.

When, in 1939, the Black Friday fires raged through the forests of valuable mountain ash, settlers did not even know how such a dominant and important tree regenerated. Sawmillers had been exploiting the mountain ash intensively for half a century, it had become 'probably the most important forest tree' in Victoria in terms of its economic potential, and people had been living at its feet and working under its canopy all their lives, yet humans did not yet know how it regenerated. It is a stunning example of how slow we can be in integrating the biographies of the trees into our management of a forest. Reading the evidence heard before Judge Stretton's 1939 Royal Commission, one is struck by the efforts made by the judge and his counsel to enquire into the science of the trees, the lives of the 'forest monarchs' that had stage-managed the event. But so little was known or distilled professionally. The academic foresters and botanists called by the Commission were born and educated overseas and were applying European models to Australian

---

52   Teague *et al., 2009 Victorian Bushfires Royal Commission Final Report*, volume 1, p. xxiii.

forests. Stretton, a local boy with great sympathy for the bush, questioned the sawmillers, landholders and local foresters and elicited some practical ecological wisdom – the mountain ash country, they told him, was different, and its fire behaviour completely distinct. But that insight was not available to him in scientific form.

It was only after 1939, following the shock of the instant economic loss of so many mature trees, that professional science began to catch up with, and to systematise, local knowledge. In the 70 years since 1939, we have lived through a revolution in scientific research and environmental understanding, we have developed the beginnings of an ecological consciousness, we have 'pried into the personal life of *Eucalyptus regnans'* (as botanist, David Ashton, put it), and we have come to a clearer understanding of the peculiar history and fire ecology of these Victorian mountain forests. The Royal Commission of 2009–10 had the benefits of that new perspective at its disposal – the ecological understanding for which Stretton sensed the need, but that no-one at that time could articulate for him.

Even though this new body of ecological knowledge has proliferated and is highly relevant to understanding fire, it has been little integrated into fire research and management itself because, as Stephen Pyne has explained, fire research worldwide has focused overwhelmingly on the physical behaviour of fire at the expense of biological and cultural studies. The physical research paradigm privileges the national over the local, and that suits governments which prefer universal management solutions.

We need more research that is deeply local, ecologically sensitive and historically informed – and that is undertaken in collaboration with the communities that live with the threat of bushfire and firestorms. All the political pressures surrounding tragedies like Black Saturday push politicians, fire managers and Royal Commissioners towards 'national' responses. Yet Black Saturday – like Ash Wednesday and Black Friday – was a fire that was characteristic not of Victoria but of a *particular region* of Victoria. To understand it fully, and to prepare for its certain recurrence, we need to come to terms with the local distinctiveness of fire. A forest is not just any forest, but a unique

community of trees with a distinct human history, and a fire is not just any fire, but one of a particular frequency, a particular intensity, a particular range.[53] What are the distinctive fire regions of Australia, and of Victoria? How will that local distinctiveness shape the behaviour of fire and people? These are simple, key questions, insufficiently studied. The value of such fire scholarship is its attention to local ecology, local history and local community. In every other way fire research should be wide-ranging: it has to be interdisciplinary, drawing on physical, biological and cultural paradigms in one holistic inquiry. But locality – expressed in the physical, geographical, biological, cultural and historical specificity of particular places or regions – should be its cohering focus. This insight has been a tragic legacy of Black Saturday, when people living in a distinctively dangerous fire region died trying to implement a blunt 'national' survival plan.

National vision has its place, of course. Accounts of firefighters struggling on the forest floor to link hoses of four incompatible threads provide a simple, clear example of where a national policy is urgent! But making fire survival plans compatible or universal or national is inappropriate and possibly dangerous. Fire is ruled by weather, ecology, topography and culture, not by jurisdictional boundaries. Yet issues of risk management, bureaucratic response, political responsibility and even charitable benevolence are jurisdictional in application and come to dominate discussion and policy formulation. Fire research needs to work against the grain of this institutional fabric and political momentum. It has to liberate and empower local knowledge and experience where it exists – and create it where it doesn't.

Fires, like floods, tend to go where they have gone before. Historical research that is also local and ecological is essential for community bushfire awareness and planning. Detailed environmental history – alert to the regional specifics of weather, geography, ecology and human settlement and management – has the capacity to integrate the physical, biological and cultural paradigms of fire scholarship.

Local fire history is also vital to active community memory, commemoration, education and participation. Whereas national institutional solutions can foster passivity in the face of a generalised fire threat, a keener awareness of local ecological and historical distinctiveness can encourage the inhabitants of fire-prone areas to be more actively engaged with managing and surviving their particular environment.

We offer this book – together with its associated study of *Black Saturday at Steels Creek* by Peter Stanley and a film about the social aftermath of the fire in Steels Creek by Moira Fahy – as a modest, integrated example of regional historical fire research done in collaboration with a local community. Another example of good local fire history is a 1984 regional study of the Blue Mountains by historian Chris Cunningham.[54] Cunningham argued 25 years ago that local fire history was 'one of the most neglected aspects of fire research' – and it remains so today. He recommended that detailed knowledge of fire history in fire-prone areas is essential not only for professional firefighters but for all households. Otherwise, 'Past fire disasters are recalled in the manner of legends or, perhaps worse still, as

53 Gill AM (1975) Fire and the Australian flora: a review. *Australian Forestry* **38**, 4–25.
54 Cunningham CJ (1984) Recurring natural fire hazards: a case study of the Blue Mountains, New South Wales, Australia. *Applied Geography* **4**, 5–27.

being preventable with modern fire suppression techniques and equipment'. Detailed local fire histories offer an important balance to the comforting contours of memory and the distorting pressures of politics. In the Blue Mountains, Cunningham observed a striking correspondence in the dates of what they call 'blow-up days' (a good example of local usage of language for special fires). By contrast with the Yarra Ranges with its concentration of firestorms in January and February, the Blue Mountains experience the most dangerous 'blow-up days' in November and December. The big fires happen in predictable weather conditions and they repeatedly attack known areas, taking almost identical paths. Local fire history has a powerful predictive capacity and is a relatively inexpensive survival manual.

Graeme Bates, Captain of the Healesville CFA, reflected after Black Saturday on the value of local memory: 'The old guys … it's handy to talk to them because they know fire behaviour, what it's going to do coming out of the mountains, how the winds react in the valleys and all that. They can tell you some good old stories of where it burnt and how it burnt and how quick it burnt, so you never forget that because it usually repeats itself … They'll say it's always come down there … and across there … and over that mountain … and that's actually what it did this time.'[55]

Historical research into the experience of fire also illuminates important questions about memory, commemoration, education and adaptation. In 2009, a National Day of Mourning was announced to mark the anniversary of Black Saturday. I hope that this significant commemorative and reflective ritual will, in the next few years, evolve into a different kind of annual event to be held on a different date. There are now many fire deaths to mourn and many different fire days to remember in Australia, particularly in Victoria – and there will be more. We need a National Fire Day that commemorates them all, but also a day that enables Australians to think and plan constructively about fire. A public holiday in the late spring could be both commemorative and practical – it would be a day to remember the power of fire, both positive and threatening, and a day to anticipate the coming summer and prepare for it.

Margaret McLoughlin, Survivors in the valley, *2011.*

55   Graeme Bates, interviewed by Rob Greaves, 25 March 2009, 'Community Living' – The Melba Project, Listen to Older Voices Studio, Healesville.

When Judge Stretton declared that bush residents in 1939 *had not lived long enough*, he was saying that lived experience alone, however vivid and traumatic, was never going to be enough to guide people in such circumstances. They also needed history. They needed – and we need it too – the distilled wisdom of past, inherited, learned experience. And not just of the recent human past, but of the ancient human past, and also of the deep biological past of the communities of trees. For in those histories lie the intractable patterns of our future. There is a dangerous mismatch between the cyclic nature of fire and the short-term memory of communities. Bushfire communities – where the material legacy of the past can never survive for long – need to work harder than most to renew their local historical consciousness. The greatest challenge in fire research is cultural.

Over millennia in Australia, Aboriginal people used tame fire to confine feral fire. 'Fires of choice,' as the historian Stephen Pyne put it, 'replaced fires of chance.' We are still engaged in that exciting and scary negotiation: what shall be our fires of choice, and to what extent can they tame our fires of chance?[56] This is a good debate to have, and my only certainty is that the best answers will be local, ecological and historical. In the wet mountain forests of Victoria and Tasmania the fires of choice are fewer and the fires of chance more fatal.

Bursting into colour

There will be more Black Days, and we have to accept them and plan for them, like drought and flood. We should aim to survive them, even if we can't hope to prevent or control them. And we should celebrate, as I think we are already beginning to do, the stimulus that such fires give to community.

In early 2011 two residents from Steels Creek jumped into a car and drove north to the Murray River to visit victims of the summer's floods in Kerang. It was a spontaneous, heartfelt sense of kinship between disaster survivors. 'The people all wore the shocked, stunned, enduring looks on their faces – which we recognised,' wrote Dorothy Barber, one of the fire survivors. 'Governments can do so much, but nothing replaces the random acts of kindness that we experienced when the volunteers turned up with help.'[57]

Steels Creek offers a microcosm of the history of settler Australia, for it has evolved from a pioneer site of rural industry to a home for commuters, retirees and farmers. As we have seen, hardly any historic buildings survive in the valley, because bushfire has swept up and down it at regular intervals – and what was not destroyed by bushfire was burnt down from the inside as domestic fire escaped. Aboriginal people, squatters, farmers, miners, sawmillers and now vignerons, weekenders and retirees have all had to learn to live with fire. A month or two after Black Saturday the people of Steels Creek didn't want any more hugs, soft toys or material things. As Roger Wettenhall would have put it, the fire for them was more than a problem in engineering – their little community had never depended much on infrastructure, anyway. They wanted help in their search for meaning, and in telling their stories. It is one of the ways that they are renewing themselves.

* * *

56   Pyne SJ (2006) *The Still-Burning Bush*. Scribe, Melbourne, p. 25.
57   Barber D (2011) Our visit to flood affected Victoria. *The Jolly Thing*, no. 90, April–May.

Contemporary Australian society, like Australian nature and like Aboriginal civilisation, will learn to see the positives about fire. We cherish the green growth that returns so quickly. We can be proud that key concepts of fire ecology and models of bushfire behaviour were developed in Australia, and that landscape-scale prescribed burning has been pioneered here as a method of bushfire management. These innovations grew from a realisation that fire was so much a part of the Australian landscape and character that it could never be eliminated and had to be lived with.

Perhaps we can even learn to see a fired landscape (of the right intensity and frequency) as beautiful – as 'clean' – as Aboriginal people do.

People who suffered in Black Saturday have surprised themselves by finding beauty in the burnt landscape. In the months after the fire survivors often said: 'I really shouldn't say this, but there's some beauty in that.' With a vertiginous and guilty sense of liberation, they could see the bones of the land and the tracts of country without 'all those fences we put in … suddenly you could see

Painting by Christine Mullen.

Margaret McLoughlin, Summer Harvest, Yarra Glen, *2011.*

forever, that great sense of space!' And it put humans in perspective too: 'It's not really about us,' reflected Margaret Houston. 'Once you see those contours of the land revealed by the fire, you realise it's a bigger story.'

Dorothy Barber said: 'After the fire, I looked at the trees and thought, "Am I going to be confronted by this blackness for the rest of my life?"' The artists in Steels Creek ground the ash into paint and made use of black leaves, burnt wire, cauterised tools and the rust from the garden shed. Even the charred trees 'are like sculptures in themselves'. Jane Calder, a member of the local Stitchers group, thought of black lace because it seemed to fringe every ridge. One painter, Robyn Henchel, said she had never bought black paint until 2009, and then went through tubes and tubes of it. Her art after the fire began with black austerity, the dark trees like prison bars (see p. 158). Then, in the spring of 2010, she introduced her first colour. By the following year her palette had exploded into wild, joyous profusion: 'This is what I see now … like a filigree, these gorgeous colours, the orange of the moss. I have burst into colour.'

Index